We Shall Remember Them

*Biographies of men associated with St. Werburgh's
who gave their lives during World War I.*

by

The Great War Study Group
of
St. Werburgh's Catholic Church, Chester.

*This book is dedicated
to the men of St. Werburgh's
who made the supreme sacrifice during the Great War
and to the families and parishioners who were wounded by their loss.*

Contents

Back cover illustration:
James McCleary, age 5, dressed for the
St. Patrick Day Concert in Chester,
17 March 1916.
Photograph by kind permission of his daughter
Mrs. Mary Powell.

Copyright © The Great War Study Group of St. Werburgh's Catholic Church, Chester.

First published in 2015 on behalf of the authors by
Scotforth Books (www.scotforthbooks.com)

Printed in the UK by Blissetts

Foreword

To wander into St Werburgh's is to enter a glorious church, the first Mass celebrated here by Cardinal Manning on Christmas Day 1875. Its Solemn Opening was on 13 July 1876, a full Haydn Mass by way of musical accompaniment.

But how much of the church we see today would have been visible then? None of the fine stained glass windows, all later additions. Edmund Kirby, our architect, was famous for his love of plain glass, with just the odd pane here and there picked out in green or yellow, to give an enchanting "off white" effect. You can see this today in the Clerestories of the church, the upper levels of windows, or, in closer detail, if you go into the Day Chapel. The High Altar? Placed there in the early 1920's as part of our Commemoration of the Great War dead. The wonderful Hanging Cross? 1933, as the date at the bottom testifies. And there are many signs of the beautiful re-ordering of the church in the first years of this century, the elegant new Altar, the re-positioning of the Pulpit, and the removal of the old Choir Stalls, all celebrated in the re-opening of the newly re-ordered church on 14 May 2002. Last, but certainly not least, the superb three-manual Binns Organ, was installed in the early months of 2004 and formally inaugurated at a Celebrity Recital on 19 June that year.

Our church then, like all others, is a study in 'change in continuity', so much the same and so much altered over time. If that is true of the fabric of our church, how much more must it be the case with the living stones of which our community is built, the men and women, boys and girls who have made up our Parish since its foundation in 1757. None of those individuals who first welcomed visiting Missionary Priests to inns and taverns in the city to say Mass in the middle of the eighteenth century are still with us: but we are their successors today, St Werburgh's Parishioners in 2015 as they were two hundred and fifty years ago. Our prayer is always the same: that we will hand on our great Parish to the next generation in at least as good a condition as we inherited it ourselves.

Who were the living stones of a hundred years ago? The Parish's Great War Group has done a magnificent job in researching the lives – and deaths – of the more than one hundred parishioners and friends of this Parish who were caught up in the First World War and made the ultimate sacrifice. But this book is so much more than their obituaries; it is nothing less than a picture of our life together a hundred years ago, and, like the church building itself, at one and the same time so recognisable and so utterly strange. The past may be a foreign country but, in this case, it is our own country, and we are proud to acknowledge it as ours.

Two of the features of the building that haven't changed over time are the Cheshire sandstone pillars on which the whole fabric rests, and the pine benches on which we sit. That is itself a symbol of change in continuity. They are the benches on which the men and women sat whose lives you will read of in this book, and to gaze at those pillars is to be transported back a hundred and forty years to the church's opening. I cannot thank the members of the Great War Group enough for their painstaking and time-consuming work in researching these lives, and for the way the whole Parish has got behind this project, with their information, ideas, suggestions and enthusiasm.

Every November, and most noticeably on Remembrance Day, we say Lawrence Binyon's words in his poem "For the Fallen":

They shall grow not old, as we that are left grow old.
Age shall not weary them, nor the years condemn.
At the going down of the sun and in the morning,
We will remember them.

In this book, I like to think we have kept faith with our Parishioners of a hundred years ago. We have remembered them.

(Fr.) Paul Shaw

July 13 2015

Acknowledgements

St. Werburgh's Great War Study Group would like to acknowledge the following persons and institutions, without whose help, this book would not have been brought to completion and publication:

Fr. Paul Shaw, parish priest of St. Werburgh's Catholic Church, Chester, for his support, encouragement and enthusiasm

St. Werburgh's parishioners who gave pictures and information

John Clark for his expert enhancing of often originally very poor quality, pictures

Cheshire West and Chester for contributions towards photocopying expenses

Commonwealth War Graves Commission for use of their memorial photographs

Brian McMahon for displaying the Group's work on the parish website

Brian Webster for the collation of material for publication

Staff at the following institutions:
    Cheshire Archives and Local Studies, Duke Street, Chester
    Chester History and Heritage, Bridge Street, Chester
    Diocese Catholique d'Amiens, France
    Diocese Catholique de Malines, Belgium
    Gonville and Caius College, Cambridge, Archives
    Military Museum, Chester
    Pembroke College Oxford, Archives
    Shrewsbury R.C. Diocesan Archives
    St. Ignatius' R.C. Parish, Sunbury-on-Thames
    St. Mary's R.C. Parish, Crewe
    Stonyhurst College Archives

Sources

Army Service Records accessed via "Ancestry"

Cheshire Trade Directories, held at Cheshire Archives and Local Studies, Chester (CALS)

Commonwealth War Graves Commission data, accessed via CWGC website

Diocese Catholique d'Amiens, France Archives

Gonville and Caius College, Cambridge, Archives

Local Newspapers covering the Great War period, held at CALS

Naval Records held at the National Archives, Kew, London

Royal Flying Corps Records held at the National Archives, Kew, London

Parishioners of St. Werburgh's, Chester

Records of H.M.S. Conway school, Liverpool Maritime Museum

Records of Overleigh Cemetery, held at CALS

Regimental Diary of the Cheshire Regiment, held at the Military Museum, Chester

Registers of St. Werburgh's and St. Francis' Parishes, and an assortment of Anglican Parish registers, held at CALS

Pembroke College Oxford, student records, held at the college

Records held by the following Guards Regiments, Grenadier Guards, Irish Guards, Life Guards and Prince of Wales' Regiment of Dragoon Guards,

St. Ignatius' R.C. Church, Sunbury-on-Thames, registers

St. Werburgh's Schools' logbooks and registers, held at CALS, Chester

St. Werburgh's Parish Magazines 1904–17, held at St. Werburgh's Church, Chester

St. Werburgh's Great War Study Group Members

John Broadhurst
Angela Clark
Norah Clewes
Walter Cunniff
Ann Marie Curtis
John Curtis
Gerald Kelly
Jan Maidment
Alan Mapp
Celia Murphy
Stella Pleass
Mary Powell
Gerard Tighe
Catherine Welsh
Harper Wright

Edward James Airth

Pte. 1st/5th Btn. Durham Light Infantry 91498

Died: 27-05-1918 age 19

Edward James, the son of William Airth and his wife Margaret nee McAndrew was born on 17 February 1899 and baptised on 19 March 1899 at St. Werburgh's. He was also confirmed there in 1909. His father William, who had been born near Bala, North Wales was apprenticed to a baker in Watergate Street, Chester. His mother Margaret had been born at Holt, Denbighshire but often visited the house of her grandparents, who lived at Parry's Entry, Foregate, Chester. William eventually became a master baker and after his marriage to Margaret in Chester, in 1884 the Airth family lived first at 13 Railway Terrace, in Chester and later at 42 Water Tower View, Hoole.

Edward had 4 elder sisters, Mary Elizabeth, Margaret Ethel, Isobel Kathleen and May Victoria Sullivan. He also had 3 younger sisters, Edith Ann, Josephine and Dorothy. His 3 brothers, one called Robert and two called William did not survive childhood. Robert and the first William died in infancy and the second William died in 1916 age 12. All the siblings were baptised at St. Werburgh's and attended St. Werburgh's Schools.

By September 1915, Edward was registered as an Assistant Postman in Chester – 188347. This was regarded at that time as a good job, being secure and with promotion prospects. Such jobs were difficult to procure and required a good reference both from school and from another well respected citizen. Edward would have been regarded by others as being fortunate.

Nevertheless Edward enlisted first with the Cheshire Regiment at Chester, on 15 January 1917, at the age of 17 years 11months. He was placed on the Army Reserves List. On 23 March 1917 he was posted to the Glamorgan Yeomanry Cyclists. On 13 April 1918 he was sent with the British Expeditionary Force to France. Here he was transferred to the Welsh Regiment at Etaples and then on 19 April 1918 he was finally transferred to the Durham Light Infantry. On 27 May 1918 he was reported missing presumed dead and later confirmed as such.

Edward's name is listed on the Soissons Memorial, Aisne, France. It is also listed on the memorials in the Town Hall, Post Office, and St. Werburgh's Church, Chester.

Edwards's medals consisted of the British War Medal and the Allied Victory Medal.

Edward's parents (Margaret died 1933 and William 1946) and three young brothers are buried in Overleigh Cemetery, Chester. Some descendants of Edward's sisters still live in the Chester area and some still attend St. Werburgh's as their parish church.

George Henry Anderson

Sapper, Royal Field Artillery, (T) 1254, Royal Engineers WR/193308

Died: 17-12-1918 age 22

George was born on 5 August 1896, the son of George Cornelius Anderson and his wife Emma nee Pritchard, who had both been born in Chester. George was the eldest of their four children, one of whom, Albert Edward had died as a child. George Cornelius had been baptised at St Werburgh's as had all his siblings. In the 1901 census George lives with his parents at 19 Charles Street, Hoole and in 1911 the parents are living at 5 Thomas Street, with two of George Cornelius' brothers, Christopher and Albert, who are unmarried. George Cornelius was employed as a stationary engine driver, in Chester. None of their three children, including George, were at home.

George's enlistment papers have not survived and so we have no details of his army service. His medal roll card shows that he did not serve abroad before 1915. It also indicates that he was transferred to the Railway Operating Division of the Royal Engineers. George died on 17 December 1918 and was buried in the Military Cemetery at Kantara, Egypt. He was entitled to receive the British War Medal and the Allied Victory Medal.

In the early part of the First World War, Kantara was an important point in the defence of Suez against Turkish attacks and marked the starting point of the new railway east towards Sinai and Palestine, begun in January 1916. Kantara developed into a major base and hospital centre and the cemetery was begun in February 1916 for burials from the various hospitals, continuing in use until late 1920. After the Armistice, the cemetery was more than doubled in size when graves were brought in from other cemeteries and desert battlefields, notably those at Rumani, Qatia, El Arish and Rafa.

Private Josiah Henry Ankers

Josiah Henry Ankers

Pte. 14th Btn. Royal Welsh Fusiliers 66100

Died: 23-08-1918 age 22

Josiah was the son of Josiah and Margaret Ankers nee Lloyd. Josiah, a bricklayer, had been born in Bunbury and Margaret was a Chester girl. The family of three girls and six boys were brought up at 8 Ingham Street. The 1911 census reveals that one sibling had died and that Josiah, who had left school, was working as an errand boy for a newsvendor.

Josiah's enlistment papers have not survived, so details of his military career are minimal but we do know that he would have been too young to enlist at the outbreak of war. His Medal Roll card indicates that he probably joined up in 1916. Josiah was killed on 23 August 1918 and was eligible to receive the British War Medal and the Allied Victory Medal. His name is listed on the memorial in Vis-en-Artois, France.

The Ankers family do not appear to have been Catholics at that stage and had no links with St. Werburgh's parish before the Great War. However, Josiah's elder brother William married Mary Thornton in 1916. She appears to have been a Catholic and later their two children, Doreen and Evelyn attended St. Werburgh's Girls' School. Another brother, John Russell Ankers married Margaret, the widow of William Stanton of this parish. The children of both these marriages were also sent to St. Werburgh's School. Richard Ankers, younger brother of Josiah, then married Winifred Callaghan of this parish, in 1929.

Albert Beckett Baker

Driver, No 1 Company A.S.C., TSR/51

Died: 21-01-1916

Albert was the son of Edwin J. and Ellen Baker nee Beckett. The family lived at 36 Beacon Street, Walsall, Staffordshire. In 1899 Albert was already in the Militia, and on 13 July 1899, aged 18 years he joined the 3rd Btn. South Staffordshire Regiment. This implies that he was born in 1881. On 28 November 1900 he was transferred to the A.S.C. at Lichfield giving his home address as Aston, Staffordshire and was sent to act as a clerk on recruiting duties at Chester. He is described on his army papers as being very satisfactory at his work. Albert remained at his posting in Chester until he was discharged on 14 November 1902 as being medically unfit. He then remained in Chester until around 1910, when he returned to Walsall.

Albert's time in Chester had not been uneventful. On 3 May 1902 Albert was received into the Catholic Church at St. Francis' Chester. Whilst in Chester, Albert also met up with Mary Ellen Stead, formerly of Aigburth, Liverpool but whose family was from Chester. Mary Ellen already had a daughter, Winifred Baker Stead. On 30 December 1903 Albert and Mary Ellen were married at St. Francis' and the family then lived in Christleton, in St. Werburgh's Parish. Two boys were born there, Laurence Carmody Baker and Terrence Hayes Baker, born in 1904 and 1905 respectively. All three of the couple's children were baptised at St. Werburgh's. Albert himself was also confirmed at St. Werburgh's in May 1905.

In the census of 1911 the whole family now live at 80 Beacon Street in Walsall, Staffordshire. Albert states his age as 34 years, thus implying that he was born in 1877. He also states that he was born in Aston, Birmingham. Albert gives his occupation as that of an artist, who is at present working as a clerk. The children are all still at school.

On 3 September 1914 Albert enlisted with the A.S.C. at Stafford, giving his age as 39 years 10 months. This would imply that he had been born in 1874. He stated that he had been 12 years in the A.S.C. or as a reservist and had been working in civilian life as a clerk. At this enlistment Albert also stated that he had been born in Tralee, Ireland. He joined the A.S.C. at Bradford.

As a former reservist Albert would have been amongst the first wave of persons sent to France. He embarked on SS Archimedes on 9 November 1914 at Southampton and disembarked at Le Havre on 13 November 1914. On 9 December 1914 he was posted to the 1st Indian Cavalry Division and from there on 5 April 1915 to the Cavalry Camp. On 11 July 1915 Albert was posted to the 1st. Div. Train where he suffered an ankle injury. On 7 July 1915 Albert was sent to England via HMS St. Patrick, arriving on 8 July 1915. From that date until 29 September 1915 Albert was treated at the Birmingham War Hospital for a fractured left leg. Albert was posted on Home service after release from hospital. On 3 December 1915 Albert was admitted to the Cambridge Hospital Aldershot where he displayed symptoms of a sore throat. This developed into cerebral and spinal meningitis, from which he died, on 21 January 1916 aged 41 years and 2 months according to his army death notification. Albert was buried in Grave R.C. 932 of Stafford Cemetery and the grave is marked with a Commonwealth War Graves Commission headstone. This gives his age as 37 years. His name is also on the Memorial Board in Chester Town Hall.

Albert was entitled to receive the 1914 Star, the British War Medal and the Allied Victory Medal. These were all sent to his wife Mary Ellen who lived at first in Foregate and later at 3 Duke Street, in Stafford.

Sergeant George Bartlett

George Bartlett

Sgt. 8th Btn. B Company, King's Own Royal Lancaster Regiment 25629

Died: 08-04-1917 age 21

His parents, George and Margaret nee Broderick, were married at St. Werburgh's on 22 June 1889. George had been born in Nottingham and was working as a railway worker. Margaret had been born in Ireland.

George was one of the middle children of the family who were brought up at 2 Reservoir Terrace, Boughton. He was born on 26 March 1896 and baptised on 26 April at St. Werburgh's. He was later confirmed there, together with his brother Thomas, in 1905. His elder siblings Joseph, Thomas, Mary, and John, and younger sister Annie were all baptised there. Sadly John died age one year and was buried from St. Werburgh's, in June 1895. Together with his siblings, George later attended the St. Werburgh's Schools. On leaving school George obtained an apprenticeship with a cabinet maker. His elder brother Thomas had gained a pupil teacher scholarship in 1905. Thomas later received Certified Teacher status and shortly afterwards enlisted, age 21. George too enlisted in 1914, age 18. In 1916, he married Edith Jane Williams in Shropshire. George served with the Expeditionary Force in France and Flanders from August 1916.

Unfortunately George's army records have not survived but certain information is known. George was killed by the bursting of a shell during the Battle of Arras (8 April 1917). His last minutes are described by his elder brother Pte. Thomas Bartlett, in the De Ruvigny Roll of Honour.

"At about 6.10pm. on Easter Sunday, George and his company were assembling to go into the trenches. While they were assembling, a German shell exploded in the cellar (where they had been billeted), killing and wounding several of George's companions. He immediately left the assembly and went down.... to help the wounded. He rescued one man and carried him up into the open streets. While he was carrying him a second shell burst in the street. It killed poor George instantly. The wounded man, however, received no additional injury."

Sgt. George Bartlett was reported killed in action in the May 1917 issue of St. Werburgh's Parish Magazine and a longer description of the circumstances was printed in the Chester Chronicle of 19 and 26 May 1917.

George was buried in Grave P. 27 at Faubourg d'Amiens Cemetery, Arras, France, Catholic rites being performed. His name is also recorded on the WW1 Memorials in the Town Hall and St. Werburgh's Church, Chester.

He was entitled to receive the Allied Victory Medal and British War Medal.

Private Hugh Beatty

Hugh Beatty

Pte. 1/5th Btn. Cheshire Regiment 3502

Died: 21-09-1916 age 39

Hugh was the son of James and Mary Beatty nee McAndrew, of Chester, who were married at the old Catholic Chapel in Queen Street, Chester on 20 October 1869. Hugh was born in Chester on 16 November and baptised at St. Werburgh's on 26 November 1876. He was later confirmed there in 1887.

Hugh was brought up in the Boughton area of Chester, with his eleven siblings. The Beatty family were one of the most loyal and active families in the parish of St. Werburgh's. As time went on different members of the family and their spouses took an active part in all parish activities, organisations and societies. The family lived originally at 43 Parry's Entry, Foregate but by 1901 had moved to 29 Victor Street.

When Hugh left school he became a bricklayer and worked for John Mayers and Son of Canal Side, Chester. He was also a well-known local amateur footballer. Hugh married Ada Baxter in Prestwich, Lancashire in September 1902 and they lived in Steam Mill Street and later at 26 Canal Side, Boughton. The couple had 6 children. The eldest Mary Ann was born in 1903 but sadly died in 1904. All the children were baptised at St. Werburgh's.

Hugh's four-figure number denotes that he is likely to have completed a short service with the Army before the start of the Great War and was then possibly assigned to the Reserves. He would then have been recalled, or volunteered, at the outbreak of war.

Hugh's enlistment papers have not survived, so little detail is known of his military service. However, we can deduce that he was involved in the gruelling action on the River Somme, France in the autumn of 1916. His date of death indicates that he was probably part of D company, which was completing work on building strong points to Gropi trench, one of the first line fire trenches. They had come under heavy enemy fire throughout their work. Having completed the work, the men were forming up when a large shell burst in the midst of the platoon. Hugh was probably one of the six who died. Seven more were wounded, of which three died later.

Pte Hugh Beatty was reported as dead in the November 1916 issue of St. Werburgh's Parish Magazine. Ada Beatty nee Baxter brought up her family in Chester and many of their descendents still live in Chester and the North-West.

Hugh was one of three brothers killed whilst on active service during WW1. Because of this tragic loss, his mother, Mary was chosen to participate in the ceremony to unveil the War Memorial on the green of Chester Cathedral, on 24 May 1922. Mrs. J. Sheriff Roberts, who had similarly lost three sons, also participated in this unveiling ceremony. Mary Beatty died a year later age 72. She apparently never reconciled herself to the fact that another son, James, who had also died in 1916, whilst doing munitions related word, never got the official recognition which came to his three brothers. Their father, James died a few months after his wife in December 1923.

Hughes' name is listed on the Memorial at Thiepval – Pier and Face 3C and 4A. It is also recorded, together with those of his two brothers, on the WW1 Memorials in the Town Hall and St. Werburgh's Church, Chester. He was entitled to the British War Medal and Allied Victory Medal.

Ldg. Seaman Peter Beatty

Peter Beatty

Leading Seaman SS 970 R.N.

Died: 23-07-1917 age 30

Peter was the son of James and Mary Beatty nee McAndrew, of Chester who were married at the old Catholic Chapel in Queen Street, Chester, on 20 October 1869. Peter was born on 25 July 1886 and baptised on 8 August 1886 at St. Werburgh's Church, Chester. He was also later confirmed there in 1899.

Peter was brought up in the Boughton area of Chester, with his eleven siblings. The Beatty family were one of the most loyal and active families in the parish of St. Werburgh's. As time passed most members of the family and their spouses took an active part in all parish activities, organisations and societies.

The family lived originally at 43 Parry's Entry, Foregate but by 1901 they had moved to 29 Victor Street. Peter left school at the age of 13 and worked as a gardener in Chester, probably at Dickson's Seeds in Newton-by-Chester. However, on 6 June 1905 he signed up for a period of 5 and 7 in the Royal Navy. This meant 5 years before the mast followed by 7 years in the Reserves. He spent 5 years service on 9 different ships before being transferred to the Royal Fleet Reserve at Devonport on 19 June 1910.

As a reservist Peter would have lived at home in Chester but done annual training with other Royal Fleet Reservists. So, in the 1911 census Peter is found living with his parents, four unmarried brothers and one unmarried sister, in the Beatty family home at 17 Victor Street. He is working as a hydraulic fitter. By 1913, when Peter acted as best man at the wedding of his younger brother John, the Beatty family had moved to 6 Beaconsfield Street. Peter's relatively untroubled life lasted until 13 July 1914, when he was called to serve on HMS Drake. In a period of leave he married "the girl he left behind him," Alice McCleary, at St. Werburgh's on 29 March 1915. The following year their daughter, Alice Mary, was born and was also baptised at St. Werburgh's.

From 8 April to 6 December 1915 Peter served aboard HMS Excellent and from 17 December 1915 to 1 December 1916 he served aboard HMS President III. This was a land-based naval facility. On 2 December 1916 Peter was with a detachment from HMS President which was sent to SS Baysarua. This ship was anchored peacefully in New Orleans harbour when Peter fell overboard, caught his head on harbour masonry and drowned in a tragic accident, on 23 July 1917. Peter Beatty R.N. was recorded as having died at sea, in the October 1917 issue of St. Werburgh's Parish Magazine. His effects were forwarded to his wife Alice who was then living at 27 Fosbrook Street, Chester.

Alice Beatty nee McCleary brought up her child in Chester and Alice Mary Beatty later became a pupil at St. Werburgh's School.

Peter was one of three brothers killed whilst on active service during WW1. Because of this tragic loss, his mother, Mary was chosen to participate in the ceremony to unveil the War Memorial on the green of Chester Cathedral, on 24 May 1922. Mrs. J. Sheriff Roberts, who had similarly lost three sons, also participated in this unveiling ceremony. Mary Beatty died a year later age 72. She apparently never reconciled herself to the fact that another son, James, who had died in 1916, whilst doing munitions related word, never got the official recognition which came to his three brothers. Their father, James died a few months after his wife in December 1923.

Peter Beatty is buried in Greenwood Cemetery, New Orleans, USA and his name is listed on a Special Memorial there. It can also be found, together with those of his two brothers, on the WW1 Memorials in the Town Hall and in St. Werburgh's Church, Chester. Peter was eligible for the Navy Star, British War Medal and Allied Victory Medal.

Greenwood Cemetery, New Orleans, USA

Richard Michael Beatty

Sapper 61st Motor Air Line Section Royal Engineers 172123

Died: 26-09-1918 age 29

Richard was the son of James and Mary Beatty nee McAndrew of Chester who were married at the old Catholic Chapel in Queen Street, Chester, on 20 October 1869. Richard was born on 29 September 1888 and baptised on 14 October 1888 at St. Werburgh's. He was also confirmed here in 1899.

Richard was brought up in the Boughton area of Chester, with his eleven siblings. The Beatty family were one of the most loyal and active families in the parish of St. Werburgh's. As time went on different members of the family and their spouses took an active part in all parish activities, organisations and societies. The family lived originally at 43, Parry's Entry, Foregate but by 1901 they had moved to 29 Victor Street.

In the 1911 census Richard is working as a gardener/nurseryman in Solihull and lodging in The Square. By 1914 Richard had returned to Chester and now ran his own successful florist, fruit and vegetable business in Frodsham Street. He advertised regularly in the monthly St. Werburgh's Parish Magazine. He married Catherine Hogan here at St. Werburgh's on 29 January 1915. Their son Edward Vincent was baptised at St. Francis in 1916 and their daughter Mary Winifred at St. Werburgh's in 1917. The family lived in Beaconsfield Street, Boughton.

Richard's enlistment papers have not survived, so little is known of his military service. However we do know that Richard apparently died of a disease contracted on a middle-east battle front. He was one of three brothers who died whilst on active service during WW1. Because of this particularly tragic loss, his mother, Mary was chosen to participate in the ceremony to unveil the War Memorial on the green of Chester Cathedral, on 24 May 1922. Mrs. J. Sheriff Roberts, who had similarly lost three sons, also participated in this unveiling ceremony.

Mary Beatty died a year later age 72. She apparently never reconciled herself to the fact that another son, James, who had died in 1916, whilst doing munitions related word, never got the official recognition which came to his three brothers. Their father, James died a few months after his wife in December 1923.

Catherine Beatty nee Hogan brought up her family in Chester. Both children attended St. Werburgh's Schools, Mary later gaining entry to Dee House Convent School.

Richard Beatty was buried in Ramleh War Cemetery, Israel and Palestine, Grave D40. His name is also listed, together with those of his two brothers, on the memorials in Chester Town Hall and St. Werburgh's Church.

Richard was entitled to the British War Medal and the Allied Victory Medal.

Walter Bird

Pte. 12th Btn. Cheshire Regiment 15307, Labour Corps 533783

Died: 12-06-1923 age 46

Walter was the son of Walter and Ann Bird nee King who had been married in the old Catholic Chapel on Queen Street on 11 February 1867. He was one of eleven siblings, Mary Ann, Thomas, Margaret, James, Ellen, Walter, William, Henry, Richard, John and George. Walter was born on 9 May 1877 and baptised on 27 May 1877 at St. Werburgh's, as were all his siblings. The family grew up at 32 Boughton. Walter snr. was a miller's timekeeper and in the 1891 census Walter jnr. had just left school, age 13 and was working as a shop boy. In 1896, Walter snr., who had latterly been working as an innkeeper in Foregate, Chester, died. His wife Ann died in 1908. Both are buried in Overleigh Cemetery, Chester.

On 26 May 1900 Walter married Elizabeth Hall at St. Werburgh's. The couple lived at 18 Pitt Street, Newtown and by 1911 they had 4 children, Walter, Nellie, Margaret and Henry. Two other children had sadly died. Also living with them were two of Walter's unmarried brothers, William and John. All three men were working as engineers on the railways. Two more children, William and George, were born to Walter and Elizabeth, in 1912 and 1914. William certainly attended St. Werburgh's Schools and it is likely that his siblings also did.

In 1914 Walter enlisted with the Cheshire Regiment, at Chester. He enlisted for three years general service on 2 September, (age according to enlistment papers of 34 years and 10 months). He had previously been working as a foundry labourer in Chester. On 6 September 1915 he embarked for France and on 28 October he was incorporated in the Mediterranean Expeditionary Force. Little of note is mentioned on his army papers except to state that Walter was transferred to the Labour Corps on 23 March 1918. He was with the 22nd Company of the Labour Corps in Salonika from 7 November 1918 to 3 March 1919. On 4 March 1919 he was sent home.

On 9 March 1919 Walter was granted leave for 28 days, then transferred to Class Z on 16 April 1919. He was discharged on 31 July 1919 at Nottingham. In January 1920 Walter's last child Richard was born in Chester and baptised at St. Werburgh's.

Walter was given a disability award for malaria which amounted to 30% disablement.

From 17 April 1919 to 2 September 1919 he had 8 shillings and 3 pence per week plus bonus. From 3 September 1919 to 8 January 1920 he had 12 shillings per week. From 9 January 1920 to 11 January 1921 he had 12 shillings per week.

In addition he was allowed 6 shillings per week for 4 dependent children from 17 April 1919 to 2 September 1919. From 3 September 1919 to 11 January 1921 he was allowed 10 shillings and nine pence for a wife and 4 dependent children.

Walter spent the last few years of his life in hospital and died on 12 June 1923 at Prince Albert Convalescent Home, Hume Parade, Worthing. His body was brought to Chester for burial in Overleigh Cemetery on 18 June 1923. Walter was eligible to receive 1914–15 Star, the British War Medal and the Allied Victory Medal.

William Joseph Bird

Pte. 1ˢᵗ Btn. Cheshire Regiment 49669

Died: 02-09-1918 age 38

William was the son of Walter and Ann Bird nee King, who had been married in the old Catholic Chapel in Queen Street, Chester on 11 February 1867. William was one of eleven siblings, Mary Ann, Thomas, Margaret, James, Ellen, Walter, William, Henry, Richard, John and George. William was born on 9 March 1880 and baptised on 11 April 1880 at St. Werburgh's, as were all his siblings. The family grew up at 32, Boughton. Walter snr. worked as a miller's timekeeper. William was confirmed at St. Werburgh's in 1895. In 1896 Walter snr. died and was buried in Overleigh Cemetery, Chester. Walter snr. had latterly been working as an innkeeper in Foregate, Chester. In 1908 his wife Anne died and was also buried in Overleigh Cemetery.

On 26 May 1900 William's brother Walter married Elizabeth Hall at St. Werburgh's. The couple lived at 18, Pitt Street, Newtown and by 1911 they had 4 children, Walter, Nellie, Margaret and Henry. Two children had sadly died. Also stated as living with them, in the 1911 census were brothers William and John. All three men were working as engineers on the railways.

William Bird enlisted with the Cheshire Regiment, at Chester on 22 March 1916. After initial training he left Southampton for France on 7 September and disembarked on 8 September at Rouen, joining the Infantry Base Depot there. On 16 September 1916 he was posted to the 13ᵗʰ Btn. Cheshire Regiment in the field and was given a new number.

On 21 October 1916 after being exposed to mustard gas, William was also wounded in action. The next day he was admitted to the 15ᵗʰ Canadian Field Ambulance with a severe wound to the neck. On 24 October he was admitted to the 4ᵗʰ General Hospital in Boulogne. It was decided that William needed to be evacuated to England and so he was taken to "St. Dennis" for transport to England. After arriving here, he was conveyed to the General Hospital in Sheffield on 18 November He remained there until 25 May 1917.

On 21 June 1917 William rejoined the 1ˢᵗ Btn. Cheshires in the field. In early October 1917 William was again affected during a gas attack and also had a severe wound to the buttock. He was treated in a local hospital, which he left on 13 October 1917. He did not rejoin the regiment until 24 October and so was disciplined for failing to return to duty as quickly as he should have done – 21 days at half pay. On 24 April 1918 William was again treated for the effects of gas and wounds and was treated in the hospital at Boulogne. He rejoined the regiment on 1 June 1918. He had a haemorrhage later that year and went into a diabetic coma in the General Hospital, Boulogne, where he died on 2 September 1918.

William was buried in Terlincthun Cemetery, Wimille, on the northern outskirts of Boulogne. He was entitled to the British War Medal and the Allied Victory Medal.

Thomas Boden

Sgt. 5th Btn. Cheshire Regiment 11891

Died: 24-05-1917 age 46 years

Thomas was born in Witton, Northwich, Cheshire the second of the three children of Thomas and Isabella (nee Canavan) Boden. The family later moved to Chester and lived at 3 Commercial Hall. Thomas' elder sister was Ada and his younger brother was Samuel.

Subsequently the family moved to 2 Love Street, where they ran a lodging house. Thomas senior died in 1882, age 59 and after that Isabella ran the lodging house herself, no doubt with help from her children.

Thomas Boden married Susannah Elizabeth Price Orrell in 1896. They lived at 2 Love Street the whole of their lives and three children, Harriet, Charles and Thomas were born there. The three children were baptised at St. Werburgh's but sadly Thomas died in 1903, age two years.

Thomas served in the Imperial Yeomanry during the Boer War 1899–1902. He was a corporal 32869 in the 21st Cheshire Company which was attached to the Yeomanry. He was discharged on 22 February 1902, due to lack of medical fitness but received the Queen's South Africa Medal, with clasps denoting action in Cape Colony, Orange Free State, Transvaal and South Africa. He then returned to Chester where he worked as a cutler from his premises at 2 Love Street. Later, in 1905 their daughter Emily was born and baptised at St. Werburgh's. Thomas' mother, Isabella had died in 1901.

When WW1 broke out, Thomas again enlisted on 10 September 1914, serving in the 5th Btn. Cheshire Regiment. He served at home during the first eighteen months but on 4 March 1916 he left for Egypt, where he stayed until 18 November 1916. He was then sent back home due to a recurrence of chronic bronchitis and was discharged as medically unfit on 1 February 1917.

He died at Chester shortly afterwards and was buried in grave G1180 at Overleigh Cemetery on 28 May 1917, Fr. James of St. Werburgh's officiating. His wife Susannah was also buried there, on 8 April 1920, in grave G1182, Fr. Porter of St. Werburgh's officiating.

An obituary of Sgt. Thomas Bo(w)den was printed in the June 1917 edition of St. Werburgh's Parish Magazine. His name is listed on the WW1 Memorials in the Town Hall and in St. Werburgh's Church, Chester. He was entitled to the British War Medal and the Allied Victory Medal.

Arthur Bradley

Sgt. 1st 5th Btn. Cheshire Regiment
354 and 240022

Died: 15-10-1918 age 28

Arthur was one of eight children born to William and Annie Bradley nee Jackson, who were married on 19 January 1874 at the Catholic Chapel, Queen Street, Chester in 1874. William was a coach smith who had been born in Glasgow and Annie was a Chester girl. They brought up their family in Chester, living first at 32 Water Tower View and later at 7 Beaconsfield Street. Arthur was born on 11 October 1890 and baptised on 30 November 1890 at St. Werburgh's, as were all his siblings.

Albert's elder sister, Agnes became a tailoress, his second sister Sarah became a photographer and a third sister Elizabeth was a theatre clerk. Arthur also had a younger sister, Edith Mary.

Arthur and his younger brother Percy were the two youngest of the family and both followed their elder brothers James and William in working at the nearby railway yards. Strangely, of the four Bradley sons, only Percy is mentioned as having enlisted, in the February 1915 edition of St. Werburgh's Parish Magazine.

Arthur's army papers have not survived, but we know from his medal roll card that he first went to France on 14 February 1915, so he must have enlisted at least in 1914. He survived some of the most arduous parts of the conflict and was in Chester on leave in February 1918. On 27 February he married Margaret Hughes at St. Werburgh's and later returned to France. Arthur was wounded, died on 15 October 1918 and was buried in Grave IV. G. I. Bucquoy Road Cemetery, Ficheux.

Arthur's name is listed on the Chester Town Hall Memorial. He was entitled to receive the 1914–15 Star, the British War Medal and the Allied Victory Medal.

Arthur Killingworth Bourne Brandreth

Pte. 23rd (Service) Btn. Royal Fusiliers, PS2492

Died: 01-11-1916 age 36

Arthur was the only child of Joseph Pilkington Brandreth and his wife Eva Jane nee Hedges. His father, grandfather and numerous other male members of both his father's and his mother's family, were Anglican clergymen. They were also people of means and did not rely on church "livings" to support their lifestyle. His father and grandfather had been educated at Eton and Christ Church College, Oxford which was the expected route for a gentleman and prospective Anglican ordinand to follow.

Arthur was born on 10 January and baptised on 15 February 1880 at the Anglican Parish Church of St. Oswald, Malpas, Cheshire, where his father, who was a curate there, performed the baptism ceremony. His early years were spent in Cheshire, living at Cuddington Lodge, Malpas, whilst his father became in turn, vicar of Shocklach and then Rector of Tilston. The family spent one year in Standish, Wigan after Arthur's grandfather died, whilst Arthur's father temporarily took over his "living." Then, when Arthur was six years old the family moved to Hove, Sussex, as his father had been appointed licensed preacher in the Diocese of Chichester. Arthur's parents continued to live in Hove for nearly twenty more years.

Arthur may first have attended a local school in Hove, before leaving to attend St. Kenelm's College. This was probably the Anglican prep. school in Oxford, which catered particularly for the sons of clergymen who desired an Anglican High Church education for their children. At the age of thirteen Arthur left St. Kenelm's to further his education. However, instead of going to Eton, Arthur became a cadet on the School Ship Conway. This was a converted sailing ship, moored in the River Mersey, near Rockferry. Here young men were educated to provide the officer class of the Mercantile Marine service. Arthur was there from September 1893 until the end of 1895, two to three years being the average period of tuition at this time. He was at Conway at the same time as John Masefield, who wrote many poems about the sea and eventually became Poet Laureate. Brandreth would also have met Laurence Kirby, nephew of Edmund Kirby, the architect. Kirby was at Conway during 1894, before leaving to go to Stonyhurst. In his naval and academic reports Brandreth is described as 'Good' or 'Fair' but he seems to have maintained rather a low profile, not being a member of any school teams or societies. On Wednesday, 19 June 1895 Arthur Brandreth was confirmed by the Anglican Bishop of Birkenhead, Bishop Royston. He had been appointed Petty Officer (a type of cadet prefect) for the Armoury at the beginning of the Autumn Term of 1894 and maintained this position until he left Conway.

Exercising his penchant for doing the unexpected, Arthur does not appear to have joined a merchant marine ship after he left Conway. Instead he became an apprenticed engineer at Messrs.

Laird of Birkenhead. Little is known of this next phase of his life but it would appear that at some stage during the next five years Arthur Brandreth was received into the Catholic Church.

In 1901 Arthur was in lodgings at 10 Charlecombe Street, Birkenhead. Then he is found working as a draughtsman for the London and North Western Railway, from 1902–04. His railway records state that he had been given a reference by Messrs. Vickers and Maxim, Barrow-in-Furness, so presumably he had worked for this firm as well as for Laird's. He may have been working for the L. &N.W.R. at Crewe, because his article on the history of plain chant, which he sent for the March 1904 edition of St. Werburgh's Parish Magazine, was sent from Crewe.

Leaving the railway drawing offices in December 1904, Arthur lived on his own means and indulged his interests in Church architecture and music. He sang at High Mass in many Catholic Churches and in 1905 was choirmaster at St. Ignatius R.C. Church in Sunbury-on-Thames, the area from which his mother's family had originated. By 1906 he was a resident of Lowestoft.

From 1904 onwards it is clear that Arthur Brandreth donated generously to St. Werburgh's Chester. It is certain that he donated a lectern and some vestments. It is also probable that he donated a cope, further sets of vestments, four small stained glass windows and a large (Assumption) window, the latter in gratitude for his reception into the Catholic Church. He probably made the acquaintance of the church architect and priest, Benedict Williamson during this time and certainly visited St. Giles RC Church, Cheadle, Staffordshire, known as 'Pugin's Gem.' He maintained a small house in Birkenhead and most probably became friendly with the whole Kirby family of Birkenhead, Edmund Kirby being the architect of St. Werburgh's Church, Chester.

In 1907 Joseph Pilkington Brandreth was appointed licensed preacher in the Diocese of Oxford, though he had taken a house in Kintbury, Hungerford, Berkshire, where he lived until his death in 1941. It may not be a coincidence that also in 1907 Arthur matriculated to Pembroke College, Oxford. However, as by now we are coming to expect, Arthur did not display the slavish devotion to his set studies as might be expected of a more normal student. He continued to study Church architecture and music in his own inimitable fashion.

By 1909 Arthur was resident in Parkfield Avenue, Birkenhead. In February 1910 Arthur Brandreth sang from the lectern in St. Werburgh's Church, Chester at the High Mass celebrated there by the Bishop of Shrewsbury, on the occasion of St. Werburgh's Feastday. In 1911 he was living in Price Street, Birkenhead.

Unsurprisingly, given the range and depth of his extra-curricular activities, it was not until 8 February 1913 that Arthur obtained his B.A. and 30 April 1914 his M.A. His B.A. was gained by the pass school examinations. These examinations were taken by those students who were deemed unlikely to achieve an honours degree. Arthur took examinations in Political Economy, History, English Literature and French.

In 1915 Arthur Brandreth was elected a life member of the Manx Society. This was an organisation which published a magazine 'Mannin' to provide Manx countrymen at home and abroad with a means of publishing matters of interest to all Manxmen, and so keep them in closer touch with each other. However, there is no obvious connection between Brandreth and the Isle of Man. His election was noted in the 1915 issue of Mannin. His enlistment was noted later in 1915 and afterwards his death in 1916.

Arthur drew up his will in 1910, well before the start of the Great War, leaving the bulk of his estate to building and other projects in Catholic Churches. He left detailed instructions concerning these projects. Many aspects of work at St. Werburgh's were to be carried out by Benedict Williamson, if he were available. If he were not, then Edmund Kirby or someone recommended by him was to complete the work.

When war broke out Arthur enlisted with the Royal Fusiliers, as a private soldier. Again, a person of Arthur's background, who also had army officers within his family, might himself have been expected to join as an officer. This was not the case. Arthur doubtless had his own reasons for enlisting in this manner but they were not made public.

Arthur's enlistment papers have not survived, so we have few details of his army career. According to St. Werburgh's Parish Magazine of January 1917, Arthur Brandreth first enlisted at the beginning of the war, with the Welsh Fusiliers. After training he was transferred to the Royal Fusiliers. His Medal Roll Card reveals that he joined the Royal Fusiliers, City of London Regiment, enlisting at Liverpool. (PS2492).

Arthur first entered France on 14 November 1915 and was killed there on 1 November 1916. This would indicate that he had been killed towards the end of the second Battle of the Somme. From September to the end of October 1916 Brandreth's Battalion was stationed at or near Raincheval, near Amiens. This area came under heavy German mortar attack due to its situation near a railhead and for other logistical factors. Arthur knew that he would be going into the front trenches in a few days time. He had already added five codicils to his will, as and when further inspirational ideas had occurred to him. On 24 October 1916 Brandreth added his sixth and last codicil. He greatly admired the lovely spire at the church in Raincheval. His codicil asked that his previous plans for a spire at St. Mary's Catholic Church, Crewe should be ignored and a spire similar to the one on the French Church, substituted. He described this new spire as progressing gradually, by small steps, towards heaven. He also altered his previous plans for St. Werburgh's. He directed that a statue of St. Werburgh in red sandstone, 5ft high be placed in the niche on the south side of the church, adjacent to the pulpit. The codicil was written on a leaf of paper torn from a notebook, witnessed and proved later to be quite legal, though, like Arthur himself, rather unusual. Arthur's unit took its place in the front trenches on 30 October 1916 and Arthur was killed there on 1 November 1916.

His obituary was printed in the January 1917 edition of St. Werburgh's Parish Magazine and his name is on the WW1 Memorial Boards of the School Ship H.M.S. Conway, Pembroke College Oxford, St. Ignatius' Catholic Church, Sunbury-on-Thames and St. Mary's Catholic Church, Crewe. He is also commemorated on the Thiepval Memorial. Arthur was entitled to the 1914–15 Star, the British War Medal and the Allied Victory Medal.

There is a memorial tablet to Arthur Killingworth Bourne Brandreth in St. Giles' Catholic Church, Cheadle, Staffordshire, the 'Pugin Gem' which Brandreth greatly admired. He left £2,000 in his will for the support of a priest at this church and also requested that his own memorial should be placed there, should he die and be buried abroad. It seems possible that his friend Benedict Williamson, who was a Catholic Chaplain during the Great War, composed the epitaph for this memorial.

Surprisingly, Brandreth's name is not on the WW1 memorial boards of most of the churches which received an endowment under his will. His somewhat grandiose plans for church building projects also proved in many cases, too expensive to be implemented using the allotted funds. However, here in St. Werburgh's we are particularly fortunate to have our lovely altar and two stained glass windows, all designed in outline by Arthur Killingworth Bourne Brandreth and installed using his bequest. Truly these are a fitting memorial to this unusual man.

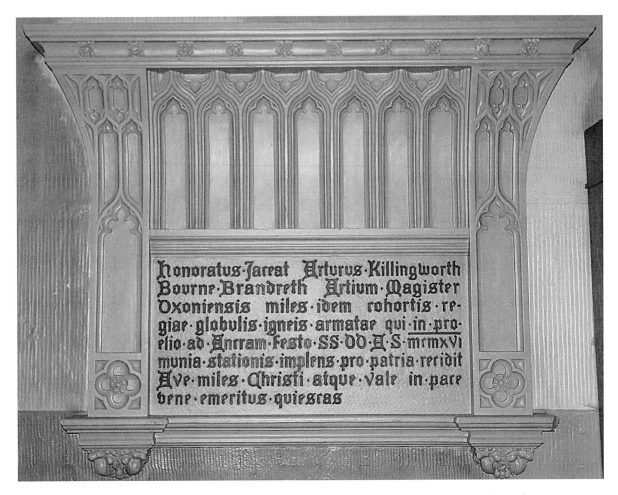

honoratus·Iaceat Arturus·Killingworth
Bourne·Brandreth Artium·Magister
Oxoniensis miles·idem cohortis·re-
giae·globulis·igneis·armatae qui·in·pro-
elio·ad·Ancram·Festo·SS·DD·H·S·mcmxvi
munia·stationis·implens·pro·patria·rccidit
Ave·miles·Christi·atque·vale in·pace
bene·emeritus·quiescas

Brandreth's Memorial Plaque in St. Giles' Catholic Church,
Cheadle, Staffordshire

Michael Philip Brown

Co. Sgt. Major A.S.C. T/752

Died: 17-06-1918 age 38

Philip was either working or being treated at the Military Hospital at Portal Lodge, Tarporley. Whilst there he received the last rites, died on 17 June and was buried on 19 June 1918 in grave 364 (Commonwealth War Grave) in the graveyard of Bunbury (St. Boniface) Parish Church. The officiant was Canon Joseph Chambers of St. Werburgh's, Chester and his burial is written in the registers of that church. However the ceremony is also recorded in the registers at St. Boniface, Bunbury, where he is buried.

It is possible that this person is Michael Philip Brown who was born to Charles and Catherine nee Cahill in Toxteth Park, Liverpool, on 27 July 1879. Charles was a seaman who had been born in Marseille, France. His son, Michael Philip Brown was baptised at St. Patrick's Church, Liverpool on 7 August 1879. He had 2 elder sisters Mary and Margaret. His younger siblings were John Thomas and Catherine. Mary had been born in Queen's County, Ireland but the remainder of the siblings were born in the Liverpool area. Michael Philip Brown may later have married Alice Rimmer and had a son George. The family were still living in Liverpool in 1911.

Philip enlisted in the King's Liverpool Regiment on 13 April 1912 and at some stage was transferred to the Army Service Corps – horse transport unit. He was discharged on 14 June 1916 as being no longer physically fit for service. He may then have been sent to the Military Hospital at Portal Lodge.

If this is the correct family, they occupied a house, Wood Villa on Bunbury Common, Tarporley from some time after 1911 until about 1920. As such they would have been parishioners of St. Werburgh's Chester. It seems likely that, after the end of the Great War, Alice married and moved from the area.

James Butler

Pte. Labour Corps 200597

Died: 20-03-1918 age 41

James was the third of nine children born to James and Catherine Butler nee Cain. His parents had been married in St. Werburgh's in 1871 and James and all his siblings were baptised here. James was born on 10 October and baptised on 22 October 1876. The family mainly lived in Swan Court, Foregate. James' sister Margaret died young and his mother, Catherine died in 1898. His brother Patrick died at the beginning of 1909. All had their requiem masses celebrated at St. Werburgh's and they were buried in Overleigh Cemetery.

In the 1901 census, the family, without Margaret or their mother, still lived together in Swan Court but in the 1911 census, the depleted family living there consisted only of James snr. John, James jnr. and Joseph. The two elder sons were nurserymen, like their father but the youngest, Joseph was an apprentice tailor. Sometime later the family moved to 23 Canal Side.

It is probable that John, James, Thomas, Raphael and Joseph Butler all enlisted in the army around 1915, though only Raphael is mentioned specifically in St. Werburgh's Parish Magazine. James' enlistment papers have not survived, so details of his army career are sparse. It appears that for whatever reason, probably illness, he was sent home at some time in 1918 and died there on 20 March. His requiem mass was at St. Werburgh's and he was buried in Overleigh Cemetery, grave 992. His brothers appear to have survived the war but their father James died in 1919. His requiem mass was at St. Werburgh's and he too was buried in Overleigh Cemetery.

James' medal roll card states that he was entitled to the British War Medal and the Allied Victory Medal. This implies that though he died at home, he had served abroad at some time.

William Patrick Butler

Pte. Cheshire Regiment 12th Bn. 33826

Died 17-09-1915 age 35

The name of Pte. P. Butler was on the original memorial plaque in St. Werburgh's. It was not on the Chester Town Hall Memorial Board.

The only possible person listed by the Commonwealth War Graves Commission is the person described below. However this person does not appear to have any connection with Chester or with St. Werburgh's Parish.

In 1911 William Patrick Butler was working as an attendant in an asylum in Abbots Langley, Hertfordshire. He was living with his wife, Mary nee Burke and his one year old son George, in one of the asylum cottages.

After war broke out William Patrick Butler enlisted with the Bedfordshire Regiment 29881, but was later transferred to the Cheshire Regiment. He was obviously involved in the Balkan campaign and was wounded. He would have been nursed at the Hospital in Sofia, Bulgaria and was buried in Grave A.4. in Plovdiv Central Cemetery, Sofia. William Patrick Butler was entitled to receive the British War Medal and the Allied Victory Medal.

Alexander Caldwell

Cpl. 5th Btn. Cheshire Regiment

Died: 1915

This man, whose details from St. Werburgh's registers are below, seems to be the only possibility.

Alexander Caldwell, born 24 August 1870 and baptised 30 August 1870

Son of Robert and Elizabeth nee Sullivan

He would be age 45 at death in 1915

Alexander Caldwell of 10 Davis Court, son of Robert Caldwell, married Martha Leech daughter of James Leech 18 May 1901 at St.Werburgh's.

An Alexander Caldwell was confirmed at St. Werburgh's in 1910.

Death of Alex Caldwell was noted in St. Werburgh's Parish Magazine.

Army records only have one Alexander Caldwell who died. He was a member of the Seaforth Highlanders and died in 1915.

His name is on the Le Touret Memorial.

Stanley Campbell

Sgt. 16th Btn. King's Royal Rifle Corps C/838

Died: 06-11-1916 age 26

Stanley was the son of John Edwin and Harriet Campbell nee Edge, of 35 Black Diamond Street, Newtown, Chester. He had an elder brother, John and a younger sister, Elizabeth. Their father John was a carpenter in Chester but sadly died in 1894, whilst the children were still young. After attending Christ Church C. of E. School, Stanley was apprenticed to his uncle Joshua West, of Dawson and West, Pawnbrokers, Chester. Later he managed the Mold branch of Mr. Dutton, Pawnbroker. He was a likeable, intelligent young man and had made a good soldier. (Chester Chronicle)

October 1914 Stanley enlisted with the King's Royal Rifle Corps. He served on the home front until 15 November 1915 and on 16 November 1915 was posted to France. Stanley had already been promoted to Sergeant by 16 August 1916 and was killed in action in France on 6 November 1916.

Stanley is described as a member of the Church of England on his army enlistment papers, attended Christ Church C. of E. School, was a member of the Church Lads' Brigade, has papers signed by the Vicar of Christ Church and at first appears to have no link with St. Werburgh's Parish whatsoever. However there is a conditional baptism for Stanley Campbell at St. Werburgh's on 8 November 1911 and he was also confirmed there on 4 February 1912. Elizabeth Campbell, his younger sister was also confirmed at St. Werburgh's in December 1912. It seems as though both siblings had converted to Catholicism. Elizabeth Campbell married James Roach at St. Werburgh's on 6 September 1913. Their three children, (one of whom was named James Stanley) were also baptised there.

Sgt. Stanley Campbell was reported killed in action in the December 1916 issue of St. Werburgh's Parish Magazine. His name is also included on the Town Hall memorial in Chester.

Harriet Campbell received her son's medals, the 1914–15 Star, British War Medal and Allied Victory Medal on 18 June 1919, when she was still living at 35 Black Diamond Street.

Sgt. Stanley Campbell is listed on the Thiepval Memorial, Somme, France – Pier and Face 13A and 13B.

Pte. John Vincent Campion

John Vincent Campion

Pte. Plymouth Btn. Royal Marine Light Infantry, Royal Navy Division PLY/17490

Died: 07-01-1916 age 19

John Vincent Campion was the third surviving child of Peter Campion, a railway worker from Shrewsbury and his wife Honoria (Norah) nee Geary, who had been born in London. John Vincent was born on 5 May 1896 and baptised at St. Werburgh's on 24 May 1896. He appears to have been called by the name Vincent in future years. By 1911 the family lived at 5 Egerton Street, Chester where Peter worked as a railway shunter at Chester Railway Station. Their eldest daughter Teresa and son Joseph worked in a restaurant, whilst Vincent worked in a boot shop. Later he became an assistant to Mr. Bithell, a butcher of Christleton Road, Chester. The younger children Genevieve and Nora were at school, whilst Pauline age 3 and Thomas age 1 were still at home. Six other children had not survived infancy. Another child Bernard, was born in March 1914. Bernard attended St. Werburgh's Schools, gaining a place at Central School in Chester when he was age 11. It is likely that the other Campion children, including Vincent, had also attended St. Werburgh's Schools but no registers from earlier times have survived.

The eldest son of the family, Joseph Peter enlisted with the 5th Btn. Cheshire Regiment, probably some time between 1911 and 1914. He entered France in May 1915 and later he transferred to the Labour Corps. From the time he entered France, until he was wounded and sent for hospital treatment at Stoke-on-Trent, Joe sent letters to the Chester Chronicle, describing the duties of the "Tommies in the trenches." They always seemed to be cheerful letters and gave news of as many Chester soldiers as possible. Joe survived the war and was discharged in March 1919.

Vincent probably enlisted in 1915 at Liverpool and after training in this country embarked with the Royal Marine Brigade on 24 June 1915, joining the Battalion at Cape Helles on 18 July 1915. Vincent was wounded at Gallipoli and was evacuated to a hospital ship. He died on 7 January 1916 and was buried at sea.

John Vincent Campion was entitled to receive the 1914–15 Star, the British War Medal and the Allied Victory Medal. His name is on the Plymouth Naval Memorial and the Memorial Board in Chester Town Hall.

John Carroll

Pte.

This is the only information which we have, from his name on the original Memorial Plaque in St. Werburgh's. There are several possibilities for regiments, but no details of these men give a link to Chester or St. Werburgh's.

There is one possible family of which John may be a member. Edward and Catherine Carroll came to live at Castle Street in Chester, from Mold, some time before 1891. They ran a lodging house here. Most of their children, including John age 16 had been born in Mold, whilst other younger ones had been born in Chester and baptised at either St. Francis' or St. Werburgh's. This seems a possible family for the John Carroll listed.

John's service record has not survived and his name is not recorded by the Commonwealth War Graves Commission.

Matthew Clayson
Australian Munitions Worker

Matthew Clayson

Australian Munitions Worker 22

Died: 01-12-1916 age 29

Matthew was born in Bradford, Manchester, England in 1887. He was the son of Matthew and Mary Ann Clayson nee Ward. The couple had been married in Prestwich, Lancashire in 1884 and the family lived at 274 Mill Street, Bradford. Matthew had an elder sister, Edith and a younger sister, Annie.

By 1901 the family had moved to 110 Gorton Lane, Manchester. Edith was a milliner and Matthew, age 14, was a trainee iron turner. Annie was still at school.

In the 1911 census the family still lives in Gorton but Matthew snr. is living in an adjacent house and Mary Ann Clayson is listed as head of the household. Matthew snr. died later that year. In 1911 Matthew jnr. was 24 years of age and was listed as an engineering fitter and gunmaker. He would have been a skilled worker as he had trained at Manchester Technical School, the forerunner of what was to evolve much later into the University of Manchester Institute of Science and Technology. His apprenticeship had been served with Sir W. G. Armstrong, Whitworth & Co. Ltd. the famous armaments manufacturer.

After his father's death Matthew decided to emigrate to Australia. He left London on 10 May 1912, aboard the Ophir of the Orient Line, with Sydney listed as his destination. He prospered in his work and the following year his mother, two sisters and his fiancée Jane McCormack joined him in Australia. Matthew and Jane were married shortly after her arrival and later two daughters were born to them. They lived in the pleasant Sydney suburb of Waverley.

Nevertheless, after war broke out Matthew returned to this country as one of the 6,000 Australian Munitions Workers who served here during the Great War. As his number denotes, he was one of the first Australians to volunteer for this work, on 30 August 1916. The voyage to Britain was uneventful, though when his ship docked in Capetown, part way through the journey, Matthew seemed to take a cold. During the journey he also struck up a friendship with fellow Australian Alfred Chambers. Their boat arrived at Tilbury Docks in London on 10 November 1916 and Clayson and Chambers made the journey to Chester on 20 November 1916 where both were to be employed at H.M. Munitions in Shotton, starting on 22 November. Whilst here they lodged with Mrs. Atkinson at 23 Cherry Road, Boughton and Matthew joined the congregation at St. Werburgh's. Matthew had still not quite managed to shake off the cold he had contracted during the voyage.

The Australians travelled by train on a daily basis, from Chester, to work at Queensferry. After only about three shifts Matthew became too ill to work. Chambers sent for Fr. Hayes, who arranged for two sisters from the Chester Convent to nurse him at home, as the rapid deterioration in his medical condition meant that Matthew could not be transferred to hospital. They were joined in their bedside vigil by Matthew's sister-in-law, Mrs. A. S. Carlon, from Manchester. Sadly Matthew died from pneumonia on 1 December 1916. He was buried from St Werburgh's, in Overleigh Cemetery, on 4 December 1916, Grave 167. It is possible but not certain that Matthew's wife and two children may have returned to this country after the end of the war.

Matthew's obituary was published in St. Werburgh's Parish Magazine of January 1917, where mention is made of his having returned from Australia to serve his country. As he did not leave Britain during the course of the war, Matthew was not entitled to receive any British campaign medals. However, as an Australian, he had gone abroad to serve his country. His grave in Overleigh Cemetery is therefore marked by and remains under the care of the Australian Section of the Commonwealth War Graves Commission.

Joseph Michael Coghlan

Cpl. "Y" 20th Trench Mortar Bty. Royal Horse Artillery 13429

Died: 19-06-1918 age 24

Joseph was the son of Patrick and Catherine Coghlan, nee Farrell, of Chester. The Farrell family was long established at St. Werburgh's. In 1871 Thomas Farrell and his wife Hannah, who were both born in Ireland, lived at 22 Railway Terrace in Chester. Thomas was a Police Sergeant and they had been living in Chester for about 9 years. Their eldest child Michael, then age 10, had been born in Ireland but 8 year old Catherine and 2 year old Charles had been born in Chester. Also living in the house was a lodger, William Healy.

In 1881 the family had moved to 7 Carter Street and Thomas had been promoted to Police Inspector. Kate was teaching in a day school and Charles was still a school pupil. This time there are 2 boarders living in the house, Patrick Coghlan an Excise Officer and Daniel Offerlehy.

Shortly after this census, Patrick and Kate were married. Their first two children John Charles and Thomas Daniel were born in Chester in 1885 and 1887 respectively and both were baptised at St. Werburgh's. Some time later the family moved to Burnley where another child Nora was born and died in 1890 age 1 year. In the 1891 census the family, consisting of parents Patrick and Kate with son Thomas, lived at 2 Hallwell Street, Burnley. Joseph was born there in 1893, his mother Catherine died there on 22 October 1893 and was buried in Overleigh Cemetery, Chester.

It seems that Patrick then moved back to Chester, with his two sons, so that their Farrell grandparents could help look after them. In 1896 Patrick married Eliza Rose Pearson at St. Werburgh's. They lived at 10 Lord Street, Chester. In 1897 their son Benjamin Patrick was born, baptised at St. Werburgh's and sadly 3 months later died. The child was buried in Overleigh Cemetery.

In the 1901 census father Patrick is living in Alloa, Scotland with his second wife, his elder son Thomas and his two daughters, Mary and Elsie. Joseph is living at the home of his Farrell grandparents with his uncle Charles, a widower, and his three children. Joseph's grandfather Thomas Farrell died in 1902 and in the 1911 census Joseph, who works as a groom, continues to live with his grandmother Hannah, his uncle Charles and his 3 cousins, at Bold Place.

As Joseph's enlistment papers have not survived, little is known of Joseph's military service. His medal roll card reveals that he entered France on 6 October 1914. Whilst there he was promoted to Corporal and also awarded the Medaille Militaire (France). He must have survived several major battles and occasions of danger before he eventually died on 19 June 1918. His effects were transferred to his grandmother Hannah Farrell.

Joseph was buried in Grave IV.D.6 in Sucrerie Cemetery, Ablain-St. Nazaire, France. He was entitled to receive the 1914 Star, the British War Medal and the Allied Victory Medal.

Private James Condon

James Condon

Pte. 1/8th Btn. King's Liverpool Regiment 3541

Died: 02-10-1916 age 44

James Condon was born in Ireland, the son of Martin and Bridget Condon of Fermoy, County Cork and married Elizabeth Mary Evans of Llanberis, Wales in 1897. James had served with the Royal Welsh Fusiliers Volunteer Battalion and entered civilian life when his term of service ended. He remained a member of the Territorial Force. James then worked for the London and North Western Railway and for 13 years was a guard, living at 17 North Street, Mold Junction near Saltney. Most of his family of seven children were born there. All the children were baptised in St. Francis' Church, Chester. After leaving the railway, James was employed as a galvaniser at John Summers, of Shotton.

By June 1913 the family had moved to 51 Francis Street, Chester, in St. Werburgh's Parish. James' wife, Elizabeth Mary was received into the Catholic Church at St. Werburgh's on 20 June 1913. James enlisted on 29 December 1914 with the 8th (Irish) Battalion of the King's Liverpool Regiment. He did service at home until 3 May 1915 when he was sent to France. On 23 May 1915 he was transferred to 176 Company, Royal Engineers. However he was described as not suitable for tunnelling work and on 25 June 1915 was returned to his former unit.

Around March of 1916 James was home on leave, for the first time and was said to be looking fit and well. He then returned to duty in France. In May 1916 James was commended for gallantry in action whilst raiding a German trench, on the night of 17–18 April. A letter from a Major-General stated that the event had been placed on record.

On 26 August 1916 James received multiple wounds to head, chest and arms. He was probably transferred to the casualty clearing station No. 21 at La Neuville. He died of gunshot wounds to the head on 2 October 1916. Pte. James Condon was reported killed in action in the October 1916 edition of St. Werburgh's Parish Magazine.

James was eligible for the Allied Victory Medal, the British War Medal and the 1914–15 Star, all of which were sent to his wife Elizabeth at 51 Francis Street, Chester on 18 March 1919. She also received his effects, which consisted of an identity disc, a pipe, a pouch of tobacco, a match box cover and a purse. She was allowed a weekly pension of 27 shillings with which to support herself and 5 dependent children.

James is buried in Grave II. D. 17 of La Neuville Cemetery, Corbie, near Amiens, Somme, France. His name is listed on the WW1 Memorials in the Town Hall and St. Werburgh's Church, Chester.

Edward Connell

Pte. 1ˢᵗ Btn. Cheshire Regiment 25229

Died: 05-09-1916 age 30

Edward was born on 11 December 1885 to Sgt. Terence John Connell, 1ˢᵗ Btn. Cheshire Regiment and his wife Norah nee Healey, at the 22ⁿᵈ Regimental Barracks, Chester. Terence John Connell had been born in Guildford, Surrey and Norah had been born in Cork, Ireland. Edward was the second youngest of six siblings, the others being Richard, Mary Ellen, William, Herbert Charles and Ada Catherine. The children were born in different towns, presumably according to their father's postings.

Sgt. Terence John Connell took part in the Chin Lushai expedition, in a region which is now part of Burma, in 1889–90. He was serving with the 1ˢᵗ Btn. Cheshire Regiment, Madras Presidency, Military No. 1276 and he received the India General Service Medal 1854, Chin-Lushai Clasp. In the 1891 census the siblings Richard, Mary Ellen, William, Herbert, and Edward were resident in the workhouse in Guildford and in December 1892 Ada Catherine was born at Elstead near Guildford.

The family later moved back to Chester and Ada Catherine was baptised in October 1894 at St. Werburgh's, Chester. In 1897 Terence John Connell died in Mullingar, Ireland. 1899 sees Edward (13) being confirmed at St. Werburgh's and his sister Mary Ellen marrying William Griffiths. On 12 August 1900 their child Mary Ellen was born and baptised at St. Francis' Chester. Edward and Ada were living with their sister Mary Ellen, brother in law William Griffiths and baby niece Mary, at 1 Greggs Court, Lower Bridge Street, in the 1901 census. On 21 August 1902 their son, William was baptised at St. Francis'. On 20 January 1903 William Griffiths started working for London and North Western Railways at Crewe. Edward joined him on 21 March 1903, with a reference from Mr. Thornhill, a wine and spirits merchant, at Lamb Stores, 2 Lower Bridge Street, Chester. In the 1911 census the Griffiths family with their four children, Edward and elder brother Richard are all living at 62 Naylor Street, Crewe. Edward is working as a porter for the London and North Western Railways. His brother-in-law, William Griffiths is also still working for LNWR. At some stage, Mrs. Norah Connell also moved to Crewe, living at 43 Naylor Street.

Soon after war broke out in 1914 Edward must have enlisted with the Cheshire Regiment. His name was on the Roll of Honour in St. Werburgh's Parish Magazine in April 1915. Edward's enlistment papers do not appear to have survived but his medal roll card states that he entered France on 13 May 1915. Sadly he was killed in action on 5 September 1916. Family members believe that this took place during the Battle for Guillemont, a particularly fiercely fought stage in the greater Battle of the Somme. Edward's name is listed on the Thiepval Memorial – Pier and Face 3C and 4A. It is also listed on the Memorial Board in Chester Town Hall. Edward's next of kin were eligible to receive his 1914–15 Star, the British War Medal and the Allied Victory Medal.

Sgt. J. Corrigan

This is the only information given about this soldier, whose name was on the original Memorial Plaque in St. Werburgh's Church. There are many dead soldiers with that surname who served in the British Army during WW1 and they are scattered across different regiments. None has any obvious ties to Chester.

The only parishioner with that surname was Mary Corrigan, who was recorded working as a servant at the Grosvenor Hotel in Chester during the 1911 census. She was from County Wexford and married Edward Walsh at St. Werburgh's in January 1914. Her father's name is stated on the register as John Corrigan. It is possible that Mary Corrigan may have had a brother who died in service during the Great War and whom she wished to have remembered.

J. Corrigan was confirmed at St. Werburgh's in 1876. This may be some relation but is unlikely to be the above Sgt. J. Corrigan.

Captain Theodore Crean

Theodore Crean

Captain, 1st Btn. Northants Regiment, latterly served with
4th Squadron Royal Flying Corps

Died: 26-10-1914 age 34

Theodore was one of 3 children and the only son, born to Dr. Richard Crean and his wife Lucy Mary nee Bolongaro, of Manchester. He was born in Manchester on the second of October, 1880 and was educated at first privately. He then went to Stonyhurst College in January 1894. There were apparently health concerns and the College was warned that Theodore might have to be taken away if the regime was too arduous. The College was also warned to notify the parents of the slightest medical indisposition. Despite this, Theodore seemed to suffer no problems during the five years he was at Stonyhurst, taking a school prize for Latin verse before he left in December 1898. He then took the Part I Examinations in June 1899 and was admitted to Gonville and Caius College, Cambridge on the second of October 1899. He took Part II Examinations in December 1899. Crean kept only three terms at Caius, throughout which he was cox of the College Boat.

During 1899 the Boer War (1899–1902) broke out and Theodore was commissioned in the 6th Btn. Lancs. Fusiliers in September 1900. He served in the South African War 1901–02, both in the Transvaal and Cape Colony. He was also at Kimberley and gained the Queen's Medal with 5 clasps. In 1902 he was gazetted to 2nd Lieut. in the 3rd Btn. Lancs. and Lieutenant in 1904. In 1908 he transferred to the Northants. Regiment and in 1911 was seconded to the West African Regiment. He obtained his company in 1913. Theodore returned to England just before the outbreak of WW1 and was co-opted to the Royal Flying Corps, 4 September 1914.

Theodore's father Richard had died in 1903 and his mother and two sisters came to live at 68, Hough Green, Chester. This was Theodore's home address when on leave. Mrs. Crean became president of the Ladies of Charity at St. Werburgh's and was also a benefactor of this church. However, Crean's younger sister, Gabrielle was married at St. Francis, Chester as Hough Green falls within that parish. She married John Allan McKenna Gillow there on 24 April 1912.

On 26 October 1914 Theodore and another officer, Lt. C.G. Hosking were on a low flying mission in a BE2 aircraft, observing the results of British artillery fire on enemy positions and signalling the information back for guidance of British artillery. They were apparently performing a very useful service, but one which entailed flying at particularly low levels. Their plane was hit by machine gun fire from the ground and crashed in flames. Both officers were interred together in a battlefield burial at Gheluvelt, between Ypres and Menin. During subsequent military action the graves were obliterated and so the two officers are listed on the Arras Memorial to the missing. Their loss, so early in the war was even more poignant as there are some indications that it may have been the result of "friendly fire."

Theodore's name is listed on the WW1 Memorials at Stonyhurst College and in the Town Hall, St. Francis Church and St. Werburgh's Church, Chester. He was eligible for the 1914 Star, the British War Medal and the Allied Victory Medal.

John Crimes

Lce. Cpl. 1ˢᵗ Btn. Loyal North Lancashire Regiment 7771

Died: 31-10-1914 age 29

John Crimes was the eldest child of John and Mary Crimes nee Kelly, who were both Cestrians. He was born in 1884 and had two younger brothers, Joseph and James. John's father was a plasterer and in 1891 the family lived at 8 Crane Wharf. Sadly John snr. died in 1892 and Mary married John Morris in 1894.

In 1901 the Crimes/Morris family lived in Harrison's Court. John was 17 years old and worked as a bricklayer. By now he had 3 younger half sisters and a fourth was born later. Sadly John Morris also died towards the end of the decade.

In 1911 the family were living at 9 St. Olave Street, except for Joseph, who had married Mary Ann Hopkins at St. Werburgh's. Joseph was received into the Catholic Church at around the same time and all John's nephews and nieces were baptised at St. Werburgh's. Later in 1911 John married Fanny Hogg at St. Michael's Church of England, though the following year they were both received into the Catholic Church at St. Werburgh's. Their two children, John and Mary were also baptised there in 1912 and early 1914 respectively. They lived at 35 Boughton and would seem to have integrated perfectly into parish life.

Then war broke out in August 1914 and disrupted their lives completely. John enlisted immediately, at Frodsham. His army number indicates that he may previously have been in the army and may in 1914 have been part of the reserves. Unfortunately John's enlistment papers have not survived and so details of his army life are rather scant. His medal roll card indicates that John was despatched immediately to France with the British Expeditionary Force, disembarking on 12 September 1914.

The 1ˢᵗ Battalion, Loyal North Lancashire Regiment was immediately involved in heavy military activity. On 13 September it lost fourteen officers and over five hundred other ranks in its first major engagement of the war, attacking up the Troyon spur to capture a sugar factory. A Regimental memorial at Troyon commemorates their sacrifice.

Those of the remaining 1st Loyal North Lancashires were then engaged in the epic First Battle of Ypres from 23 October, when they made a most gallant and successful bayonet charge at the Kortekeer Cabaret. They then took part in the desperate fighting around Gheluvelt on 31 October, remaining in action until 14 November.

On 31 October 1914 John Crimes was killed in action, most probably in the fighting near Gheluvelt. His name is listed on the Ypres, Menin Gate Memorial, Panel 41 or 43. He was eligible for the 1914 Star with clasp, the British War Medal and the Allied Victory Medal. His name is listed on the Memorial Boards at St. Francis, St. Werburgh and the Town Hall in Chester.

Private Patrick Cunniff

Patrick Cunniff

Pte. Kings Shropshire Regiment, transferred to
Royal Warwickshire Regiment 203830-260200

Died: 24-09-1917 age 34

Patrick was born in Creggs, County Galway, Ireland on 29 November 1882. He was one of a family of 4 sons and a daughter. Patrick and his older brother Andrew came to England in the early 1900's and settled in the Boughton area of Chester. Patrick married Margaret Geraghty, a dressmaker who lived in Steven Street, at St. Werburgh's in October 1907. Their first child, Mary Josephine was born in December 1909 and she was baptised at St. Werburgh's in January 1910. Their son John was born in 1912 and was also baptised at St. Werburgh's. During this time the family lived at 118 Francis Street and Patrick was employed by Mr. Burley, of Hoole Bank Brickworks.

Patrick's enlistment papers have not survived, so little is known of his period in the army. However, it is known that he took part in the 3rd Battle of Ypres, generally known as Passchaendale. Pte. Patrick Cunniff was mentioned as having been killed in action in the November 1917 issue of St. Werburgh's Parish Magazine. According to a letter sent on 28 September 1917 by the Army Catholic Chaplain, Patrick had been shot as he entered the trenches and died instantly. He was buried on the battlefield, behind the lines the following day. In the Chester Chronicle of 20 October 1917 it stated that Patrick's Captain, Priest and Army Chaplain had all expressed admiration for Patrick's previous conduct and bravery. He was entitled to receive the British War Medal and the Allied Victory Medal.

Patrick's two children were brought up in Chester by their mother, Margaret, but sadly Mary Josephine died, due to cardiac problems, age 13. However, their son John (Jack) lived until his sixties. He married Catherine Carrig at St. Werburgh's on 17 June 1944, wearing his WW2 RAF uniform. Jack died in the 1970's but has family who still live in the Chester area.

Patrick Cunniff is buried in Grave IV.B.43 Brown's Copse Cemetery, Roeux, Pas de Calais, France. His name is listed on the WW1 Memorials in the Town Hall (spelling incorrect) and St. Werburgh's Church, Chester.

Private Joseph D'Arcy

Joseph D'Arcy

Pte. 1st Btn. Royal Welsh Fusiliers 18199

Died: 18-07-1916 age 23 years

Joseph was the son of Daniel and Margaret D'Arcy nee Kelly. Daniel had been born in Ireland and Margaret was from Holywell, Flintshire, where the couple were married in 1883. Their first two children were born in Flintshire and the next two were born in Ireland. The couple then moved to Chester, where Daniel worked as a foreman gardener at Dickson's Seeds Ltd., Newton by Chester. They settled here and brought up the rest of their family in Chester. As they changed addresses in Chester, the children were baptised either at St. Werburgh's or St. Francis. Daniel John was born in Chester in 1891 and baptised at St. Werburgh's. Joseph was born on 9 April 1893 and baptised on 21 April 1893, at St. Francis. Sadly their mother Margaret died in 1895 and the following year Daniel married Leah Woods, in Chester. Six more children were born to the family, including Amelia in 1904, who died the same year.

In the 1911 census Daniel John and Joseph are living with their father, stepmother, and half siblings William, Hugh, Robert, Elizabeth and Richard at 110 St. Anne Street, Chester. Joseph age 17 is working in the Messrs. Davies tobacco manufacturers, Canal Street, Chester.

Joseph first enlisted with the 9th Battalion of the Cheshire Regiment, at Chester, on 31 August 1914. He was discharged on 8 October 1914 as being unlikely to make an efficient soldier. Undeterred, he enlisted with the Royal Welsh Fusiliers on 25 November 1914 and remained with them throughout his military career. His enlistment papers for the Royal Welsh Fusiliers have not survived and so there are few further details of his service. However it is known that he was wounded, treated and returned to service, prior to the engagement on the Somme which caused his death. (Chester Chronicle).

Pte Joseph D'Arcy was reported killed in action in the September 1916 issue of St. Werburgh's Parish Magazine. His name is listed on the Memorial Boards in Chester Town Hall, St. Peter's Church and St. Werburgh's Church. He was entitled to the 1914–15 Star, the British War Medal and the Allied Victory Medal.

Joseph is buried in Grave III. C. 13 Flatiron Copse Cemetery, Mametz, Somme, France.

George Dobbins

Pte. 8th Btn. Cheshire Regiment 31067

Died 29-01-1917 age 29

In 1873 Thomas Dobbins and Mary Flaherty of Great Budworth were married in Northwich. They attended St. Wilfred's Catholic Church there and most of their family, including George, were baptised there: John, Thomas, Richard, Bridget, twins William and Mary, John , Michael, James and George. Sadly the eldest John, then Bridget and Mary, all died in childhood.

By 1891 the family had moved to Chester, where their youngest child Mary Ann was born and later baptised at St. Francis. The family lived in the Lower Court area and were involved in the rag and bone and bottle dealing trades. By 1901 the family had re-located to Birkenhead and though Thomas and Richard had left home, the rest of the family continued in the bottle dealing trade. In 1911 Thomas and Mary were back in Chester, living with youngest daughter Mary Ann, in Seaville Street. Thomas was in the scrap iron and bottle dealing business, whilst the two women were cloth cutters.

Meanwhile George married Alice May Ford at St. Nicholas Parish Church, Liverpool, in 1908. The couple lived at 69 Dacre Street, Birkenhead and George continued in bottle dealing. The couple had four children, Charles Thomas, George, Daisy, and John Arthur. The family lived in Back St. Ann Street and the children were baptised at St. Laurence's Birkenhead. Sadly the eldest child died before his first birthday

On 23 September 1914 George and Alice had a Catholic marriage ceremony at St. Laurence's Birkenhead and shortly afterwards George joined the Army Reserves. On 11 April 1916 he enlisted from the Reserves and on 10 September 1916 he joined the Mediterranean Expeditionary Force. George was successively part of the A.S.C. the King's Own Shropshire Light Infantry (24374), the 17th Reserve Bn. Cheshire Regiment and finally the 8th Bn. Cheshire Regiment. His family continued to live at 61 Back St. Anne Street, Birkenhead, after George's enlistment.

George served in the Asian Theatre of War and died in Mesopotamia on 29 January 1917. He was probably involved in the recapture of Kut al Amara. This action began 13 December 1916 and ended with the taking of Kut in February, leading to the taking of Baghdad in March, 1917. George's name is listed on the Basra Memorial. He was entitled to receive the British War Medal and the Allied Victory, Medal.

Thomas Dobson

Lce. Cpl. 1ˢᵗ Btn. Royal Welsh Fusiliers 4499

Died: 28-08-1916 age 25

Thomas was the youngest child of William and Mary Dobson nee Bunnell of Chester. Thomas was born around December 1890 and at that time his father worked as a fisherman. His older brothers George, John and William became fish sellers. Thomas also had an elder sister, Mary Elizabeth. The family were Anglican. Sadly Thomas' parents William and Mary died in 1903 and 1905 respectively.

In 1910 Mary Elizabeth married James McCleary a widower, father of three young daughters and a stalwart parishioner of St. Werburgh's. Thomas made a home with his sister and her new family in Canal Side, Chester, where his brother-in-law was an assistant to a marine store dealer. Thomas himself worked as a rag-gatherer.

Thomas married Elizabeth Hewson in Chester, in March 1914 and when war broke out, enlisted at Wrexham. Thomas' number and his swift deployment into France indicate that he may have been in the army before, or that he was in the Reserves or Territorials. By 6 October 1914 Thomas was serving in France. However, Thomas must have been in Chester, in January 1915, because both Thomas and his wife Elizabeth were received into the Catholic Church at St. Werburgh's that month. Their son Thomas Ypres Dobson, who was born in February 1915 was also baptised at St. Werburgh's, Mary McCleary (possibly Thomas' sister), being the godmother. Her husband James had enlisted by this time with the Royal Field Artillery but was discharged for medical reasons at the end of July, later that year.

Anecdotal family information states that Thomas may have been suffering from a gas attack and recuperating at home during the early months of 1915. Thomas later returned to France.

Because his army enlistment papers have not survived, it is difficult to reconstruct his final days. Pte. Thomas Dobson died on 28 August 1916, presumably as a result of operations on the Somme. Here, on 1 July 1916, French and Commonwealth forces launched an offensive on a line from north of Gommecourt to Maricourt. Despite a preliminary bombardment lasting seven days, the German defences were barely touched and the attack met unexpectedly fierce resistance. Losses were catastrophic and with only minimal advances on the southern flank. The initial attack was a failure.

In the following weeks, huge resources of manpower and equipment were deployed in an attempt to exploit the modest successes of the first day. However, the German Army resisted tenaciously and repeated attacks and counter attacks meant a major battle for every village, copse and farmhouse gained. At the end of September, Thiepval was finally captured. This village had been an original objective of 1 July. Attacks north and east continued throughout October and into November in increasingly difficult weather conditions. The Battle of the Somme finally ended on 18 November with the onset of winter.

Thomas' death was reported on the Roll of Honour in the November 1916 issue of St. Werburgh's Parish Magazine. Then, Fr. Maurice Hayes, the priest who had received the Dobson family into the church, went back to the register and wrote R.I.P. in large letters at the side of Thomas Dobson's conditional baptism entry.

Thomas was entitled to receive the 1914 Star with clasp, the British War Medal and the Allied Victory Medal. His name is listed on the WW1 Memorials in the Town Hall and in St. Werburgh's Church, Chester. Thomas' name is also listed on the Thiepval Memorial, Pier and Face 4A.

Edmund Francis Dodsworth

Lce. Cpl. London Regiment Royal Horse Artillery (London Rifle Brigade) 2305

Died: 02-07-1916 age 41

Francis was the second son of George Edmund Dodsworth and his wife Penelope Ruth nee Wilford. He was also the nephew of Mrs. Amelia Barker nee Dodsworth of Heron Bridge, Eaton Road, Chester. Mrs. Barker was the wife of Henry Yates Barker, a Chester solicitor. Mrs. Barker worked very hard for Parish, City and War efforts. The Barker family were responsible for many donations to St. Werburgh's Church, including in 1893 that of the baptismal font which is still used today. They may have had a particular regard for St. Werburgh's, as Amelia Barker was the sister in law of its architect, Edmund Kirby. Mrs. Barker also made donations of money and goods, in order to equip the Convent in Union Street to treat up to 10 resident wounded soldiers. The nursing sisters there had originally only limited room for hospitalised cases. They normally treated few such persons, concentrating on a free dispensary and outpatient treatment centre, for the poor of Chester. As the toll of war injured mounted, the places at the Union Street Convent were gratefully used, mainly by evacuated Belgian wounded.

Francis was the second son of Mrs. Barker's brother, George Edmund Dodsworth. It seems strange that Francis, the son and grandson of professional military officers, should enlist as a private soldier. However, that appears to have been the case. His army records have not survived and so no details of his army career are available. Lance Cpl. Francis Edward Dodsworth was reported killed in action in the August 1916 issue of St. Werburgh's Parish Magazine. Mrs. Barker also placed a notice of her nephew's death in the Chester Chronicle. Francis Dodsworth was entitled to receive the British War Medal and the Allied Victory Medal. He was buried in Doullens Communal Cemetery, Extension Number 1. Edmund Francis Dodsworth is one of the few Anglicans who are listed on St. Werburgh's Memorial Board.

Richard Donnelly

Lce. Corporal, Military Police Corps, Military Foot Police P/3849

Died: 27-03-1917 age 29

Richard was born in Chester on 1 January 1888 and was baptised in St. Francis on 12 January of that year. He was the son of James and Mary Ellen Donnelly nee Clancy. His father was a bricklayer and the family lived in the Northgate area of town. Richard lived with his parents and three elder siblings, Margaret, Walter and James, and one younger sister Elizabeth. Sadly their mother died between 1891 and 1901. This seems to have caused the family to split up. In 1901 James snr. is lodging with one family in the Northgate area and his sons Walter and Richard are lodging with another family, in whose business both brothers are working. Although only 13, Richard is working as an assistant to a cart driver. It is possible that he was later employed at Chester Leadworks.

Richard married Constance Eva Evans in a civil ceremony and their sons Walter and Albert were born in 1909 and 1912 respectively. In 1912 the family were living at Clare's Court, Charles Street, Hoole and in 1913 both children were baptised at St. Werburgh's.

On 31 August 1914 Richard enlisted with the Cheshire Regiment at Chester, age 26 years 8 months. His service lasted only 2 months. He was discharged as medically unfit on 30 October 1914. Undeterred by this event Richard applied to the Royal Welsh Fusiliers at Wrexham. He enlisted on 10 May 1915. This time his service lasted an even shorter time. He was discharged as medically unfit on 19 May 1915.

Richard and Constance's third son John Edward, had been born on 7 February and baptised on 14 March, 1915 at St. Werburgh's. On 18 June 1915 Richard and Constance had a religious marriage ceremony at St. Werburgh's.

Sometime after this event Richard was accepted by the Military Police Corps and served until illness overtook him. He died in the Military Hospital, Newport, whence he was conveyed to Overleigh Cemetery, Chester, where his body was buried in Grave Number G1163. Fr. Maurice Hayes of St. Werburgh's officiated. As Richard did not serve abroad, he would not have been eligible to receive campaign medals.

John Draycott

Pte. 11ᵗʰ Btn. Cheshire Regiment 52695

Died: 23-11-1918 age 23

John was the seventh of fourteen children born to Charles and Sarah Ann Draycott, nee Hill. The couple lived in the Boughton area of Chester and their family was brought up there, often living at different houses in Steven Street. Later in their married life Charles and Sarah converted to Catholicism and so like most of his siblings, John was baptised at St. Werburgh's in 1902. After leaving school, John found employment with the firm of Williams and Gamon, Victoria Road, Chester. The 1911 census finds the family living at 39 Steven Street.

John enlisted with the 5ᵗʰ Btn. Cheshire Regiment, at Chester on 6 March 1916, age 19. He was at home until 18 July 1916, when he was posted to France with the British Expeditionary Force. In France, John was transferred to 11ᵗʰ Btn. Cheshires. By 12 March 1918, the 11ᵗʰ Cheshires were stationed at Berkeley Camp, Bihucourt. From 21–23 March 1918 the 11ᵗʰ Cheshires were involved in withstanding a major German offensive. They were moved forward to strengthen the line, being put in gaps between other divisions, sent to re-establish a Corps line which had been broken and so on. Orders were sometimes rescinded part way through being carried out and the situation was fluid to say the least, in the area of the Vaulx-Beugnatre road. Casualties were high and often groups of men were captured as they made their way to trenches or positions behind abandoned former front lines. It is probably under these confused circumstances that John was taken prisoner.

John was released at the Armistice but had by then developed pneumonia and on 18 November 1918 was admitted to L' Hopital Auxiliaire de l'Armee No. 6, La Malorange near Nancy. Five days later, on 23 November 1918 he died. His father received his commemorative plaque, scroll, British War Medal and Allied Victory Medal, on 3 December 1920.

John's elder brother, William also lost his life in this conflict.

John is buried in Grave 54 Jarville Communal Cemetery, Meurthe-et-Moselle, France. It is the only British grave in a military plot of 69 French graves and 3 Indian graves. It is also listed on the WW1 memorial in St. Werburgh's Church, Chester.

William Draycott

Pte. 1st Btn. Grenadier Guards 13430

Died: 11-10-1917 age 27

William was the third child and second son of Charles and Sarah Ann Draycott, nee Hill. The couple lived in the Boughton area of Chester where they brought up their family of fourteen children. Later during their married life Charles and Sarah converted to Catholicism and as a result most of their children were baptised at St. Werburgh's in 1902. William may have missed this family baptism as he was a boarder at the Industrial School in Chester at about this time. When William enlisted in the Grenadier Guards in 1907 the family lived at 5 Seaville Buildings but later they moved to 12 Steven Street and in the 1911 census they were living at 39 Steven Street.

William joined the Grenadier Guards on 23 October 1907 in Chester at the age of 18 years 6 months. He enlisted for a short service which meant 3 years with the Colours and 9 with the reserves. On 10 October 1910 William extended his service to complete 7 years with the Colours. During this time he served only at home.

On 8 November 1914 William joined the British Expeditionary Force in France and was to serve there for 3 years. William was wounded during the Crossing of the Broembeek, with others of the 1st Battalion. He died at 47 Casualty Clearing Station, on 11 October 1917. Pte.William Draycott was reported killed in action in the November 1917 issue of St. Werburgh's Parish Magazine.

William is one of two brothers, who lost their lives in this conflict and was entitled to receive the British War Medal and the Allied Victory Medal, in addition to the 1914 Star with clasp.

He was buried in Grave 54, Dozingham Military Cemetery, West-Vlaanderen, Belgium and his name is listed on the WW1 memorial in St. Werburgh's Church, Chester.

George Farrell

Pte. 1st Btn. Royal Welsh Fusiliers 5137

Died: 11-12-1914 age 18

George was born in Chester, the son of James and Jane Farrell nee Baker and was baptised at St. Werburgh's Church. Both parents were in the tailoring trade and the family had previously lived in different parts of Northern England, notably Newcastle under Lyme and Birkenhead. In Chester the family lived in Davies Court, Love Street. George's father James died in 1905 age 54 and was buried in Overleigh Cemetery. His mother Jane continued to work as a tailoress and by 1911 was living in Parkes Court, Love Street, most of the family having left home. Only the eldest daughter Bertha, Joshua Septimus, and George were at home. George was 15 and working as an errand boy.

George enlisted just after the outbreak of war but his enlistment records have not survived, so we know few details of his military career. What is certain is that he arrived in France on 2 November 1914 and was killed one month later, in those confused early days of WW1. Trenches had become a feature of the Great War after the Battles of Aisne and Marne, in the autumn of 1914. From the 1st Battalion's War Diary we know that during early December the 1st Battalion of the Royal Welsh Fusiliers had been billeted in Rue Biache, where George probably joined them. On the 8 December they returned to the trenches. On the 11 December, 2nd Lt. Jerman was wounded in an unsuccessful attempt to carry off an enemy's detached port. In this same action one other ranking soldier was killed and two were wounded. George was probably the other ranking soldier mentioned as being killed in this action.

George Farrell was listed as killed in action in the February 1915 edition of St. Werburgh's Parish Magazine. He was entitled to receive the 1914 Star, the British War Medal and the Allied Victory Medal.

George's elder brother, James also died in this conflict.

George's name is listed on the Ploegsteert Memorial, Hainaut, Belgium, Panel 5.

It is also listed on the WW1 Memorials in the Town Hall and St. Werburgh's Church, Chester.

James Farrell

Pte. 2nd Btn. Royal Welsh Fusiliers 7969

Died: 25-10-1914 age 33

James was born in Birkenhead in 1881, the son of James and Jane Farrell nee Baker. Both parents were in the tailoring trade and the family had previously lived in different parts of Northern England, notably Newcastle under Lyne (where they were married) and Birkenhead. Sometime after 1891 the family moved to Chester, where they lived in Davies Court, Love Street. James snr. died in 1905 age 54 and was buried in Overleigh Cemetery. His wife Jane continued to work as a tailoress and by 1911 she lived in Parkes Court, Love Street with most of the family having left home.

James had joined the regular army, enlisting for six years with the Cheshire Regiment on 30 August 1901 age 19 and was involved in the Boer War. He served in South Africa from 23 January 1902 until 3 October 1902. He gained the Queen's South Africa Medal with clasps for service in the Orange Free State and Cape Colony.

On 29 October 1903 he transferred to the Royal Welsh Fusiliers and on 26 November 1906 he transferred to the reserves, now giving his civilian address as Parkes Court, Love Street, Chester.

As a reservist James would have been recalled immediately war broke out, if not before. His younger brother George also enlisted with the Welsh Fusiliers in September 1914. Both brothers were sent to France very early in WW1. James arrived there on 11 August 1914 and died there on 25 October 1914. In an internal note, his commanding officer wrote saying that his medals were to be sent to his joint legatee, his brother George. At the time of writing the officer would not have known that by now George also had been killed.

Jane Farrell received her son James' medals, the 1914 Star with clasp, the British War Medal and the Allied Victory Medal, in 1920, when she was living at 88 Malden Road, Chester.

James is buried in Grave XI.C.3 of the Pont-du-Hem Military Cemetery, La Gorgue, France. His name is also listed on the WW1 Memorial in the Town Hall, Chester.

Thomas Feeney

Pte. 5th Btn. Cheshire Regiment 1534

Died: 29-04-1915 age 22

Thomas was the eldest son of Michael and Winifred Feeney nee Clancy, of 28 Steven Street, Boughton, Chester, who were married at St. Werburgh's in 1890. Michael was a railway worker. Thomas was born on 13 July 1892 and baptised at St. Werburgh's on 7 August 1892. He was later confirmed here in 1905.

Thomas had eight siblings, Catherine, James, Robert, Mary Ellen, Michael, Edward, Winifred and Annie. Thomas and James are not present in Steven Street on the 1911 census, so may be working elsewhere. They may even have already joined the army.

Thomas' enlistment papers have not survived, so little is recorded of his army history. However, a letter received after his death and published in the Cheshire Observer on 22 May 1915, reveals that Thomas trained in Northampton and was billeted at 112 St. Leonard Road, Far Cotton, during his training. The householder had written to the Feeney family to express his regard for the fallen soldier and sent condolences to the family.

Thomas' medal roll index card reveals that he served in France from 15 February 1915 and was killed in action there on 29 April 1915. He was probably one of the two men killed on that day, in the frontline trenches of the Kruisstraat sector, due to enemy sniping. Seven others were badly wounded and three slightly wounded.

Thomas was therefore entitled to the 1914–15 Star, together with the British War Medal and the Allied Victory Medal. His death was reported in the June 1915 edition St. Werburgh's Parish Magazine.

Thomas is buried in Grave I. F. 8 Spoilbank Cemetery, West-Vlaanderen, Belgium. His name is on the Memorial Board in Chester Town Hall and in St. Werburgh's Church.

Lance Corporal Isaac Field

Isaac Field

Lce. Cpl. 490th Field Company Royal Engineers 7555

Died: 26-02-1919 age 31

Isaac Field was born in Boughton in 1888, the son of Robert and Esther Field who were market gardeners in the area. He had 3 elder brothers, Robert, William and Oliver. In 1911 he married Winifred Frost, first in a civil ceremony and later in St. Francis' Church, Chester. Thereafter they lived with the Frost family at 14 Vernon Road. Isaac was working as a fireman with the Great Central Railway at Chester and by the start of the Great War the couple had two small children, Elizabeth and Esther Ann. Elizabeth was baptised at St. Francis' and Esther Ann at St. Werburgh's. Both attended St. Werburgh's Schools.

Isaac enlisted soon after the start of the war and served in France from 23 October 1915. He was wounded during the summer of 1918 and was nursed in a French hospital. Eventually he was repatriated to the War Hospital in Chester where he died one week later on 26 February 1919. He was given a military funeral on Tuesday 4 March 1919 and was buried in Grave 4068 Overleigh Cemetery.

Isaac was entitled to receive the 1914–15 Star, the British War Medal and the Allied Victory Medal.

Thomas Fox

Pte. 13th Btn. Welsh Regiment 285225

Died: 26-04-1918 age 20

Thomas was the youngest child of Michael and Ann Fox. Michael was born in Caernarvonshire and Ann was born in Shrewsbury. Michael had joined the Militia at a young age and in 1871 was billeted, with three other Militia men, with the Jones family who lived near Mold. Ten years later Michael was a patient in a military hospital at Stoke Davenport. It is possible that he married Ann Done in early 1875 at Manchester. In the 1891 census they are living at Gresford and have four children, Julia, Ann, Katie and Michael. Michael snr. is working as a tin miner and it appears that he has moved around the country since he left the Militia, as his children are born in Neston, Wilmslow, Oswestry and Penymynydd respectively. Peter was later born at Rossett, then Maggie and Thomas were born at Holywell.

Sadly Thomas died in Wrexham in 1899 age 44 and his widow moved with the children, to Chester. First they lived at Parry's Entry and later at 57 Steven Street. Ann worked as a licensed hawker to support her family. Her youngest son Thomas enlisted with the 7th Battalion of the Cheshire Regiment at Chester. His enlistment papers have not survived, so we have very few details of Thomas' army career. At some stage he was sent to France, possibly early in 1916. It was probably here that he was transferred to the Welsh Regiment. Thomas died on 26 April 1918 and was buried in Grave I.D.15 at Bagneux Cemetery, Gezaincourt.

Thomas was entitled to receive the British War Medal and the Allied Victory Medal. His name is listed on the Memorial Board in Chester Town Hall.

James Gaffney

Pte. Welsh Regiment 16813

First disembarked France 15-07-1915

Discharged 09-06-1916

This is the person who best fits the Pte. J. Gaffney whose name was on the original Memorial Plaque at St. Werburgh's. This James Gaffney may have died after his discharge, due to a war related illness.

He may be related to Thomas Francis Gaffney who married Eleanor Newns at St. Werburgh's in 1909 and lived at 93 Westminster Road, Hoole.

James Garvey

Pte. Royal Defence Corps 30312

Died: 02-07-1917 age 51

James, the son of Thomas and Bridget Garvey nee Riley, was born in Chester on 17 October 1865 and baptised at St. Werburgh's on 29 October 1865. He grew up in Steven Street and was already working as a general labourer at the age of 15. As a young man he first joined the Cheshire Regiment (20043) and served in the Burma and South African Campaigns.

James married Mary Callaghan at St. Werburgh's, Chester on 8 July 1893. They lived at various addresses in Boughton, Chester and their children were born here and baptised at St. Werburgh's. In the 1901 census James is away, possibly on army duties and Mary lives in Charles Street with her three daughters. By 1904 the family lives in Fosbrook Street and by the 1911 census James is back home and appears to have left military life. He may have been transferred to the reserves.

His military records have not survived, so few details of his WW1 service are available. However it states on his medal roll index card that he enlisted on 8 September 1914 and was discharged due to sickness in accordance with paragraph 3G2 XVI of King's Regulations, on 4 July 1917. However, anecdotal reports state that during WW1 he experienced a severe gas attack and as a result he was transferred to the Royal Defence Corps, a unit which protected military installations in this country. James later died.

James was buried in Grave 1121 of Overleigh Cemetery, Chester on 6 July 1917. His name is listed on the WW1 Memorials in the Town Hall and St. Werburgh's Church, Chester. James' wife, Mary was buried in an adjacent plot, Grave 1124, in Overleigh cemetery in 1928.

As you can see, the dates given by the different sources, conflict with the date of death given by the Commonwealth War Graves Commission and used at the top of this entry.

Private Peter Gerrighty

Peter Gerrighty

Pte. 10th Btn. Cheshire Regiment 59637

Died: 13-01-1918 age 37

Peter was the eldest son of James and Catherine Gerrighty nee Kelly, who had married at St. Werburgh's on 13 October 1878. Though James had been born in Ireland he was living at Parry's Entry, Chester and Catherine who had been born in Chester, lived in Steven Street. The couple then set up home in Hop Pole Court, Foregate, Chester. Their first child Bridget was born in 1879 and baptised at St. Werburgh's but sadly died the following year and was buried in Overleigh Cemetery. Of their other children, Peter and Margaret were born in Birkenhead, and Mary Ann, Catherine, Martin and Sarah in Stockport. In 1891 the family lived at 1 Dickenson's Court in Stockport and appears to have attended St. Joseph's Church there. The family then appears to have lived alternately in Steven Street, Chester or Lloyd's Court, Stockport. We can assume that these migrations were caused by James' work as a bricklayer. James died in Stockport in 1906 and his widow Catherine then permanently settled the family back in her home town of Chester, at 59 Steven Street.

Peter's civilian and military life was nothing if not interesting during this period. On 4 November 1897, age 17, Peter had enlisted with the 3rd Battalion of the Cheshire Regiment, number 4269, to serve for six years. He had been working as a labourer with Messrs. Galloways and Co. of Manchester and had lived at 9 Talbot Street in Stockport for the previous year. At this time the rest of his family was living at 17 Steven Street, Chester. On 6 December 1898 Peter enlisted in Manchester with the Royal Irish Fusiliers, 6418. At this time his family was living in Stockport and Peter joined the regiment at Colchester on 7 December. Life in the Royal Irish Fusiliers did not seem to suit Peter and he absented himself for a week on two separate occasions. This resulted in his having to serve two periods of a fortnight in army prison. On 26 June 1901 he was stated as having deserted. On 25 November 1902, at the age of 20 years and 10 months, Peter enlisted at Manchester, with the Royal Horse Artillery, 29200. In his enlistment form he stated that he had previously served with the Cheshire Regiment but that his time had expired. The family was living at 17 Steven Street at this time. His fraudulent enlistment was quickly uncovered and he was imprisoned for 20 days before being discharged for misconduct on 1 January 1903. No doubt Peter thought or hoped that this would be the end of his army days.

Peter married Ann Caldwell in Chester in 1905 and the couple set up home in Steam Mill Street. In Jan. 1910 their daughter, Margaret Ann was born and baptised at St. Werburgh's on 6 February 1910 but sadly she died in 1911.

After the Great War broke out, despite any misgivings which he may have had, Peter enlisted with the 10th Battalion, Cheshire Regiment. This time his enlistment papers have not survived. All we know of his Great War service is that he died on 13 January 1918 and was buried in Favreuil British Cemetery. He was eligible to receive the British War Medal and the Allied Victory Medal. Peter's name is listed on the Town Hall Memorial Board in Chester.

Alfred John Gibson

Cpl. 1ˢᵗ Btn. Life Guards 2916

Died: 13-05-1915 age 20

The Gibsons were an old Chester family. Alfred's grandfather Michael was first a solicitor's clerk and later a newspaper reporter in Chester. Sadly both Michael and his wife Ann died in the early 1870's leaving a family of 6 children. In the 1881 census their son Alfred George Gibson, age 16, was working in a bakery and lodging with a family in Pipers Ash. Alfred George Gibson married Elizabeth Meakin in 1886 and in the 1891 census they were living with Elizabeth's mother and their two children, Alfred John and Mary Elizabeth, in Birkenhead. By 1901 the family had moved to Haydock but in 1904 Elizabeth died. Alfred George re-married in 1905 and by 1911 Alfred John was working as a newspaper reporter in Warrington, whilst his sister, Mary Elizabeth was working as a servant at Notre Dame Blackburn Girls Convent School. The "Haydock" Gibsons still had many "Chester" Gibson relations with whom they appear to have kept in close contact.

Alfred was 18 years old in 1912 and working as a cub reporter on a Warrington newspaper, when he enlisted on 29 August with the First Battalion of the Life Guards, at Warrington. He gave his place of birth as Haydock, near the town of St. Helens. Alfred was a giant of the times, being over 6ft 1 inch in height and was considered fit for service in the Household Cavalry Corps. He was signed for a short service, i.e. eight years with the colours and four with the reserves and 2 days later actually joined the Household Cavalry at Windsor. During 1912 he gained his third and then second class Army Certificates of Education and seemed to be set for a successful army career.

Alfred's army service was at home until 14 August 1914, when he joined the British Expeditionary Force to France, still with the rank of Trooper. Alfred would have taken part in the action around Mons and Le Cateau but lived to form part of the re-organized B.E.F. the following year. On 20 January 1915 he was promoted to Corporal. Alfred was killed in action on 13 May 1915 at Potijze. It appears that the enemy started shelling his position at 0330 hr. and from 0400 to 0700 hr. the shelling was unabated. Thereafter it continued all day. The casualty returns for the 1ˢᵗ Life Guards that day were: Killed 24, Wounded 58, Missing 11. Alfred would have been one of the 24 who were killed.

Cpl. Alfred Gibson's death was recorded in the August 1915 edition of St. Werburgh's Parish Magazine. He was entitled to receive the 1914 star, British Empire Medal and Allied Victory Medal. Instead, his father and sister Mary Elizabeth would have received these, together with other effects, at their home at 13 Blackbrook Road, Haydock.

Alfred's name is listed on Panel 3 of the Ypres (Menin Gate) Memorial, West-Vlaanderen, Belgium. His name is also recorded on the WW1 Memorials in the Town Hall and in St. Werburgh's Church, Chester.

Joseph Gough

Pte. 3rd (Prince of Wales's) Rgt. of Dragoon Guards D/5984

Died: 06-06-1915 age 26

Joseph was the eldest child of Henry and Elizabeth Gough nee Chambers, who had married in Henley, Oxfordshire in 1888. Elizabeth was an elder sister of Canon Joseph Chambers, who was rector at St. Werburgh's during the Great War.

Joseph was born in Hambledon, Buckinghamshire but lived with his family in Henley and later in Reading, Berkshire, where his father was a butcher.

By 1911 Joseph aged 22 had enlisted with the Dragoon Guards and was stationed at Barossa Barracks, Aldershot. Before the Great War started he saw service with the regiment in Egypt and in August 1914 Joseph would have been with his battalion in Cairo. From here they were recalled to England. They arrived at Liverpool on 18 October 1914 and by 31 October 1914 had landed in France. It seems possible that Joseph Gough could have paid a visit to his uncle and namesake during the short interval when the regiment was in this country.

On 4 November 1914 the 3rd Dragoon Guards came under the command of the 6th Cavalry Brigade in the 3rd Cavalry Division. This unit had been fighting relentlessly during what came to be called the first Battle of Ypres. Joseph joined them in time to take part in the last Battle of Nonne Bosschen on 11 November before winter operations took over.

On 11 May 1915 the Battle of Frezenburg Ridge marked the start of the 2nd Battle of Ypres. Joseph was killed on 6 June 1915 and was buried in Grave I.e. 142 of Bailleul Communal Cemetery extension, Nord, France. His obituary was printed in St. Werburgh's Parish Magazine of July 1915. Joseph Gough was entitled to the 1914 Star, the British War Medal and the Allied Victory Medal. His name is on the WW1 memorial in St. Werburgh's Church, Chester.

Private Thomas Goulding

Thomas Goulding

Pte. 1/5th Btn. Cheshire Regiment 2728

Died: 10-10-1916 age 20

The Gouldings were a prominent Catholic family resident in Tarporley. Martin Goulding, an Irishman had settled there in the mid-nineteenth century and with his first wife Mary nee Hunter started a chandlery business in the High Street. Their children Martin, Mary, Elizabeth, Peter and Michael were born there and baptised at St. Werburgh's, Chester. Sadly Mary died soon after their son Michael was born and Martin later married Catherine Hanley. They too raised their family in Tarporley. George Goulding, the first son of this second marriage, was baptised at St. Werburgh's in December 1863. The Goulding children were well educated, the girls being sent as boarders to Notre Dame Convent in Manchester. As they grew up, the girls tended to take up teaching and the sons started their own businesses in Tarporley. By 1914, Tarporley High Street had four stores or businesses, each owned and operated by different members of the Goulding family.

Martin's son, George married Emma Coates in Chorlton, Manchester in 1893. They proceeded to run a gentlemens' outfitters and tailor's shop at 54 High Street, Tarporley and most of their children, Martin, George, Thomas, Catherine, Patricia, Frederick and Winifred were born there. However, some time between 1902 and 1905 George Goulding and his family relocated their business to 10 Linen Hall Street, Chester, whilst they lived in Queen Street. Their youngest son, John Joseph was born here in 1906 and baptised at St. Werburgh's.

Ironically, the attic of their former house and business premises in Tarporley was then used as a Mass Centre. Starting in November 1906, a priest from St. Werburgh's went there each Sunday to say mass for the few (mainly Goulding) Catholic locals, whose ranks had been swollen by an influx of about 20 Irish grooms, who came regularly with their employer, the horse breeder and trainer, J. J. Maher, for the Tarporley hunting season. Some of the Goulding cousins were baptised in this Mass Centre, though their baptisms were registered at St. Werburgh's Church, in Chester.

Thomas (Tom) Goulding, George and Emma's third son attended St. Werburgh's School and then became apprenticed to Messrs. Rowley and Sons, watch makers and jewellers, Cow Lane Bridge, Chester. He was apparently well thought of by his employers who also described him as a 'favourite with the firm's customers.' At the age of 18 he joined the Citizen Volunteers at Mollington, where he won second prize for shooting. Tom was apparently a keen Volunteer and used to ride from Chester to Mollington to drill. Mollington was the birthplace of the Volunteer movement in this country. Tom's death was the second of a man originally from this unit. Tom also distinguished himself six months before his enlistment by jumping fully clothed into the canal to rescue a child. (Chester Chronicle)

In 1912 Thomas' elder brother George had left his position with a tea merchant in Chester and had enlisted with the Territorials for a 4 year stint. His eldest brother Martin, who had worked in his uncle's pub, the Forester's Arms in Tarporley, also enlisted later. It would have been no surprise to his parents therefore, when Thomas enlisted with the Cheshires in October 1914 at the age of 18 years and eight months. Thomas' enlistment papers have not survived and so his army history is ill documented. However in his obituary (Chester Chronicle of November 1916) it states that Thomas had been at the western front for fourteen months and had taken part in several big battles, without being hit, until he was wounded on 7 October 1916. The 5th Cheshires had been utilised in pioneer working parties, in an area of the Somme valley south of Montaubon, from 1–10 October and several men were wounded each day. Six soldiers of other ranks were wounded on 7 October; Tom died of his wounds on 10 October 1916.

Thomas is buried in Grave I. J. 45, Grove Town Cemetery, Meaulte, Somme, France.

Pte. Thomas Goulding was reported as dead in the November 1916 issue of St. Werburgh's Parish Magazine and his name is listed on the WW1 Memorial Boards in the Town Hall and in St. Werburgh's Church, Chester.

He was entitled to the 1914–15 Star, the British War Medal and the Allied Victory Medal.

Francis Green

Lce. Cpl. Cheshire Regiment 9459, Labour Corps 265299

Died: 22-02-1919 age 26

Frank Green was born in 1893, the son of Edward Burrell Green and his wife Annie. Frank had an elder stepbrother Richard, an elder brother William, two younger sisters Nellie and Daisy and a younger brother Charles. Frank had been born in Wellington Shropshire but his siblings had been born in many other northern areas, as his father's work as a contractor took him to different parts of the country. In 1901 the family lived in Wenlock but it appears that later they moved to Cheshire.

Frank enlisted with the Cheshires on 3 June 1910, stating his occupation as a groom, and served at home until 5 October 1911. There then followed 3 years in India, until the Great War broke out. The Cheshires were sent back home and on 9 December 1914 Frank joined the British Expeditionary Force. He arrived in France on 16 January 1915 and remained part of the B.E.F. until 10 July 1915, before being transferred to the Labour Corps. Frank had been sent home on 11 April 1915 due to ill health and remained on home duties thereafter. After some time he was diagnosed as having contracted tuberculosis due to exposure to extreme conditions in the trenches near Ypres. He was discharged on 13 December 1917.

During this time at home, he had married Elizabeth Jankinson nee Harnott, widow of John Jankinson who is also listed on this memorial. Frank now had a wife and stepdaughter Kathleen Elizabeth and in 1917 a daughter of his own Edna May. Edna May Green was baptised at St. Werburgh's in September 1917 when the family were living at 13 Milton Street.

Frank's illness deteriorated rapidly towards the end of 1918 and he died at the Royal Infirmary in Chester, having received the last rites. He was buried in Grave 1123 of Overleigh Cemetery on 26 February 1919. Frank was entitled to the 1914–15 Star, the British War Medal and the Allied Victory Medal.

Joseph Hall

3rd Steward Mercantile Marine SS Diomed (Liverpool) 1126

Died: 22-08-1915 age 16

Joseph was an orphan and was adopted as a young child, by Mary and Patrick Whelan. Patrick was a cooper, and the family lived at 47 Boughton, Chester. The Whelan's had no children themselves and would have been able to provide Joseph with a comfortable home. Joseph was confirmed at St. Werburgh's in 1910.

Mary Whelan died in 1912 age 58 and was buried from St. Werburgh's in Overleigh Cemetery, on 6 June, Fr. Hayes officiating. Later Joseph decided that he wanted to go to sea. He entered the mercantile service in Liverpool. His address on entering the service was 468 Price Street, Birkenhead.

Joseph left Liverpool on board the SS Diomed, which had been built in 1895 by Scott's of Greenock. They were en route to Shanghai, when on August 22 1915 they were sunk by German Submarine U38, 57 miles WNW of the Scilly Isles. Joseph Hall's body was lost at sea. Patrick Whelan died two years later, in Chester age 56 and was buried from St. Werburgh's, Fr. Rope officiating.

Joseph Hall's name is listed on the Tower Hill Memorial, London. It is also listed on the WW1 Memorials in the Town Hall and St. Werburgh's Church, Chester.

Albert Edward Hargrove

Lce. Cpl. 15th Btn. Cheshire Regiment 52439

Died: 26-03-1918 age 35

Albert was the son of Edward and Margaret Hargrove, who were both born in Ireland, as were Albert and five of his siblings. Edward was a regular soldier in the British Army and by 1891 was a Colour Sergeant stationed at Colchester Barracks.

By 1901 Edward had retired from the army and worked as a clerk in Chester, the family living at 17 Tomkinson Street. Albert was sixteen years of age and working as a printing compositor. By 1911 the family of parents and eight children lived at 132 St. Anne Street. One child had died and two more had left home. Albert's two younger sisters were teachers at the St. Werburgh's Schools and his two younger brothers were clerks, one in the civil service and the other in a solicitor's office. Twins Katie and Ruth May, age 13 were still at school and three year old James had no specific occupation.

Albert's enlistment papers have not survived though his medal roll card states that he was eligible to receive the British War Medal and the Allied Victory Medal.

Albert was buried in grave III. J. 10 Beacon Cemetery, Sailly-Laurette, France.

James Harvey

Unfortunately we have no further information about this man, except that he was named on the original memorial plaque in St. Werburgh's, with the rank of private. He is not listed on the memorial board in Chester Town Hall.

Sergeant Thomas F Heaney

Thomas Francis Heaney

Sgt. Royal Engineers 45644

Died: 02-06-1918 age 50

Thomas Heaney was born on 29 October 1867 and baptised 10 November at St. Werburgh's. In 1881 he was also confirmed there. He was the son of Patrick and Bridget Heaney nee Heveran of Chester. The family lived first in Steven Street and later at 5 Fosbrook Street.

On 15 September 1895 he married Catherine Feeney, daughter of Michael Feeney, at St. Werburgh's. The couple lived at 5 Fosbrook Street and later at 53 Steven Street, Chester and brought up their family of 8 children there. All the children were baptised at St. Werburgh's and attended St. Werburgh's School. Thomas worked as a general labourer.

In the December 1914 edition of St. Werburgh's Parish Magazine, where the surnames of volunteers are listed, it states that two members of the Heaney family have enlisted. It appears that both Thomas and his eldest son James, who would have been just eighteen, have both volunteered by this time. Thomas definitely joined the Royal Engineers and it is possible that James also joined this regiment, becoming a signaller. Family anecdotal evidence states that Thomas volunteered at an enlistment event in City Road. It is impossible to envisage the feelings of Catherine Heaney at this time, having both her husband and her eldest child volunteer for the army during wartime.

Thomas' enlistment papers have not survived, so details of his army service are minimal. However, his Medal Roll Index card reveals that he entered France on 5 September 1915 and served for some time at the front. He was home on leave in May 1918 and did not feel well. On Monday 27 May he went to the Central War Hospital in Chester. An operation was performed but Thomas did not survive it. He died there having received the last rites.

A Requiem Mass was held at St. Werburgh's on 6 June. Then, according to the Chester Chronicle of Saturday, 8 June 1918, Thomas was buried in Overleigh Cemetery, with full military honours. The Cheshire Regimental Band played the 'Dead March' and four fellow NCO's carried the coffin, which was covered by the Union Jack, to the grave. Rev. C. James conducted the service and the 'Last Post' was sounded. Sergeant Heaney's youngest child, Agnes, was not listed as a mourner but she lived in Chester until her death in October 2014 and could remember seeing her grandmother, Thomas' mother, wearing a black bonnet to go to the funeral.

Thomas' son James possibly served in the Balkan theatre, at Salonica. He survived the Great War, married and brought up a family in Chester. Thomas' younger children were brought up in Chester by their mother and all prospered. Perhaps the most successful of them was Mary Heaney, who became Sheriff of Chester in 1959/60 and Mayor of Chester in 1964/5.

The Heaney family are unusual, in that both father and son were on active service in the British Army during the Great War.

Thomas Francis Heaney was entitled to the 1914–15 Star, the British War Medal and the Allied Victory Medal.

He is buried in grave 992 of Overleigh Cemetery, Chester. His name is also listed on the WW1 Memorials in the Town Hall and in St. Werburgh's Church, Chester.

Richard John Hennessey

Lce. Cpl. 2nd Btn. South Lancs. Regiment 2314

Died: 27-07-1915 age 40

Richard was born in 1875, the son of Richard and Emily Hennessy of Clerkenwell, Middlesex, London. He was one of the older children of the twelve born to the couple. Richard grew up in London, where his father worked as a bottler for a soda water producer. By 1881 Richard snr. had moved to a shop in the corporation buildings in Clerkenwell, where he was registered as a mineral water manufacturer. Sometime before 1891 the whole family moved to 2 Ayr Villas in Stamford, Lincolnshire. Richard snr. now worked as a foreman at a mineral water works in Stamford, with Richard jnr. age 15 also working as a drayman and George Frederick his brother, working as a messenger boy.

Richard and his brother George Frederick, who was only 18months younger, seemed to be particularly close but by 1901 their paths had diverged. Though both trained as engineers, Richard was working at Chatham Naval Docks, Kent and George had come to work as a railway engineer in Chester and was living in lodgings at 10 Lord Street. In Chester, George met and married Edith Ellen Williams, daughter of William Vaughan Williams, at St. Werburgh's, on 19 July 1902. The couple set up house at 2 Garden Terrace, Spital Walk, Boughton. By 1911 four children had been born to them, all were baptised at St. Werburgh's but sadly two had died. Another son Maurice Bernard was born and baptised here in June of 1913.

Meanwhile, George and Richard's parents, Richard and Emily, had retired but still lived in Stamford, at 13 All Saints Place, with their two youngest sons, Thomas and Vincent, who were employed in local foundries and machine workshops respectively.

Richard enlisted with the South Lancs. Regiment in Manchester, on 21 August 1914. It states on his enlistment form that Richard had previously been a member of the 4th Battalion, Lincolnshire Territorials and had seen service in South Africa. Unfortunately we have not been able to find any details of this service.

On 22 October 1914 Richard joined the British Expeditionary Force to France and Flanders and on 16 December 1914 he was promoted to Lance Corporal. Sadly Richard was killed in action on 27 July 1915 at St. Eloi and at first was given a battlefield burial there. Later he was re-buried in Grave IX.B.1. Enclosure No.3, Voormzeele Cemetery, West-Vlaanderen, Belgium, 2 miles south of Ypres. Notice of the death of Pte. Richard John Hennessy of S. Lancs Reg. was placed in the September 1915 issue of St. Werburgh's Parish Magazine. His name is also listed on the WW1 Memorials in the Town Hall and in St. Werburgh's Church, Chester.

Richard and George's father had died and so Richard's effects were sent to his mother Emily, at 13 All Saints Place, Stamford, Lincolnshire, on 24 March 1916. They consisted of a belt, gloves, notebook, identity disc, scapula, correspondence, stationary, silver watch and tobacco. Emily Hennessy had moved to 4 Church Lane, Stamford by November 1921, when she received the 1914–15 Star, British War Medal and Allied Victory Medal which had been awarded to her son.

George Hennessy was a benefactor of St. Werburgh's Church and no doubt asked for his brother's name to be placed on our memorial. Another child was born into the Hennessy family in Chester on 1 November 1917. He was named Lawrence St. Eloi Hennessy. Sadly he lived for only two months.

William Thomas Hudson

Pte. Royal Welsh Fusiliers 46113

Died: 20-12-1916 age 31.

William was the son of Amos and Mary Hudson nee Green and was born in Chester in 1885, where he was baptised at St. Francis. He was later confirmed at St. Werburgh's in 1899.

William was brought up at 29 William Street and later worked as a French Polisher with a piano manufacturer, Messrs. Herbert Ellis and Co., of Chester. William's mother Mary died in 1911 and in 1913 his sister Mary married Walter Edward Jones. At the outbreak of war, William lived at 13 Clare Avenue, Hoole with his father Amos, sisters Mary and Esther and brother in law Walter.

William married Mary Cotgreave at St. Werburgh's in 1914 and they lived at 61 Cherry Road. Their son, Romuald William was born the following year and baptised at St. Werburgh's.

At the end of the year, on 4 December 1915 William enlisted in the Royal Welsh Fusiliers. In 1916 he was sent to Mesopotamia and would have been involved in (unsuccessful) attempts to relieve Kut-al-Amara. Empire troops at Kut surrendered at the end of April 1916. On 1 January 1917 William was reported missing. On 17 July 1917 he was presumed dead. In St. Werburgh's Parish Magazine of September 1917, it states that 'Pte. William Hudson previously reported missing is now reported killed in action.'

The details behind the bald entries on the army record of Pte. William Thomas Hudson, were provided at a later court of enquiry. The court convened at Bombay Hospital, where Cpl. Gough, an inmate was to give evidence. According to the account of Cpl. Gough, Pte. Hudson had been shot by a sniper, in the neck or shoulder, whilst their unit had been trying to cross the River Tigris at Hussaini, on 20 December 1916. Pte. Hudson fell and was not seen to move again. The rest of the unit was pinned down by heavy fire and eventually had to retreat.

Pte. Hudson's wife Mary, of 61 Cherry Road, Chester received his plaque, scroll and medals in 1920.

Pte. William Thomas Hudson's name is on the Basra Memorial, Panel 15. His name is also listed on the WW1 Memorials in the Town Hall and St. Werburgh's Church, Chester. He was entitled to the British War Medal and the Allied Victory Medal.

A. F. Hughes

Lt.

Died: May 1917

The death of Lt. Hughes is mentioned in the May 1917 edition of St. Werburgh's Parish Magazine. No other details were given. His name is not on the Town Hall Memorial and was not on the original memorial at St. Werburgh's.

It is possible that he was the Frank Hughes previously referred to as organising musical evenings at the Young Catholic Mens' Club of St. Werburgh's Parish.

He could also be the F. A. Hughes who sang from the lectern with Arthur Brandreth at the High Mass on St. Werburgh's Feastday in February 1910.

There was also a Mr. Hughes who was choirmaster at St. Werburgh's in 1916.

Exhaustive searches of the registers of both St. Werburgh's and St. Francis' Churches and examination of Chester census material has revealed no-one of suitable age. Neither did searching available army records.

It is possible that Hughes did not live in Chester but still led St. Werburgh's Choir.

It is also possible that Hughes was a relation of the choirmaster.

George William Hughes

Pte. 12th Btn. Cheshire Regiment 9035

Died: 20-10-1918 age 29

George William Hughes was the son of John and Mary Hughes of Boughton, Chester. He had an elder sister, Ada and younger siblings John, Ann, Martha, Kate, and Albert. The family lived at 45 Seaville Street, and later in Back Brook Street. George was confirmed at St. Werburgh's in 1905. He enlisted with the Cheshires on 17 June 1908 when he was 18 years 7 months.

George's pre-war service was at home and in India, where he spent four years. When war broke out the Cheshires were recalled from India, George with them and then sent onwards to France on 16 January 1915. George was at home during the latter part of 1915 through to 14 September 1916, when he embarked for Salonica. He was reported missing on 15 April 1918 and proved to have been taken prisoner of war. In a repatriation process after the Bulgarian capitulation in September 1918, George was sent to a British Military Hospital at Philippopolis, where he was treated for pneumonia but sadly died. He was buried in grave A.5. Plovdiv General Cemetery, Sofia, Bulgaria.

The Commonwealth servicemen buried at Plovdiv Central Cemetery died either as prisoners of war or while serving with the occupying forces following the Bulgarian capitualtion in September 1918. It was formerly called Philippopolis (St. Archangel) Cemetery and was formed after the Armistice by the concentration of graves from the following sites :- Philippopolis Protestant Cemetery; Philippopolis Roman Catholic Cemetery; Karagatch Protestant Cemetery; Kostenecbanja British Cemetery; Kurtova Konare Civil Cemetery; Mustafa Pasha British Cemetery and Tatar Pazardzik Protestant Cemetery. The cemetery now contains 55 Commonwealth burials of the First World War.

George was eligible to receive the 1914–15 Star, the British War Medal and the Allied Victory Medal.

Private John Hughes

John Hughes

Pte. 1st/4th Btn. Prince of Wales' Volunteers
South Lancashire Regiment 4922, 202507

Died: 12-07-1917 age 28.

Patrick and Ellen Hughes nee Stanton were married at St. Werburgh's in 1888. Patrick had been born in Ireland and Ellen had been born in Chester. The couple set up house at 29 Steven Street and Patrick worked as a seedsman and gardener, probably at Dickson's Seeds in Newton-by-Chester. John was the eldest of their four children, born on 19 June 1889 and baptised 7 July 1889 at St. Werburgh's. He was later confirmed here in 1905. John's three younger siblings Thomas, Mary Ellen and Francis were also baptised at St.Werburgh's. By 1911 John was no longer at home, Thomas was employed at the lead works in Chester and Mary Ellen was in domestic service. Frank was still at school. Mary Ellen attended St. Werburgh's Schools and it is probable that all the siblings did so.

It appears that John may have enlisted with the South Lancashire Regiment well before the Great War. His original four digit number indicates such. He is certainly absent from the 1911 census, when the family are living at 29 Steven Street and would have been old enough to have joined the army by that time. His mother Ellen died in Chester on 25 December 1914 being buried from St. Werburgh's and it is possible that John's grandmother, Ann Hughes then acted as housekeeper for the family, as the youngest member, Frank would still have been a schoolboy. John listed his grandmother Ann Hughes as his sole legatee.

John's enlistment papers have not survived so we know little of his army career. However, we do know that he is unlikely to have entered France before 1916. He fought only in France and Flanders and was wounded in 1917. He died of wounds on 12 July and was buried in Grave XV. B. 8A. at Lijssent Military Cemetery, 12km west of Ypres, in West Flanders, Belgium. Pte. John Hughes was reported as dead in the August 1917 issue of St. Werburgh's Parish Magazine.

John was entitled to receive the British War Medal and the Allied Victory Medal. His name is listed on the Town Hall Memorial Board in Chester.

Frederick Hull

Lce. Cpl. 25th (Tyneside Irish) Btn. Northumberland Fusiliers 59315

Died: 23-03-1918 age 25

Frederick was the elder of two sons born to William and Elizabeth Hull nee Rice, who were married at St. Francis' Church, Chester in January 1892. By 1901 the family lived in Eastgate Row and William was employed as a cabinet maker's assistant. Sadly Frederick's brother Albert was at this time in the isolation hospital on Sealand Road. Albert recovered from his illness and was at home for the next census in 1911, when the family lived at 3 Brassey Street in Hoole. William was now a furniture salesman and both his sons were working as clerks, Frederick in the probate office and Albert in a brewery.

Both brothers had been baptised at St. Francis' Church. It is possible that Frederick and Albert had also attended St. Francis' School and certain that as young men they joined St. Francis' Club, even though they were now living in St. Werburgh's parish. The Chester Chronicle of 20 May 1918 stated that Frederick and his brother were musicians, Frederick specialising in piano and Albert in violin. Frederick was also a keen sportsman and rower, being one of the four who won the Eaton Plate at Chester Regatta in 1914.

The enlistment papers of neither brother have survived, so we can know little of their army careers. Frederick's medal roll card indicates that he served abroad after 1915 and so was entitled to receive the British War Medal and the Allied Victory Medal. He died in March 1918 and his name is on the Arras Memorial.

John Ernest Harrison Jankinson

Pte. 2nd Btn. Royal Welsh Fusiliers 10703

Died: 09-05-1915 age 23.

John was born in 1892, the eldest child of James Ernest Harrison Jankinson and Frances Elizabeth nee Clarke. The family lived at 34 Hartington Street, Handbridge Chester and in the 1911 census John and his three younger brothers and two younger sisters are all living at home. John age 19 was working as an electric crane driver. He married Elizabeth Harnott in Chester in September 1912 and the couple set up house at 13 Milton Street.

John's enlistment papers have not survived but from his Medal Roll Index Card, we know that when war broke out John enlisted at Liverpool and by 6 October 1914 was in France. John died at the beginning of May 1915. In a letter sent by G. O. Thomas, Captain Commanding A Company and published in the Cheshire Observer of 15 May 1915, John was stated as having been killed instantaneously by a shell, at the start of a big attack initiated by the English army in the early morning.

John's daughter, Kathleen Elizabeth Harrison Jankinson was born on 1 June and baptised at St. Werburgh's on 6 June 1915, one month after her father's death. Kathleen's mother Elizabeth later married Francis Green at St. Werburgh's. Kathleen later gained a half sister, Edna May Green. In January 1919 Francis Green also died as a result of illness contracted in the trenches during the Great War. Kathleen spent a year at St. Werburgh's Girls' School, where her guardian was listed as her maternal grandmother, Mrs. Magee. She left the school in March 1924, when the family left Chester.

John gained the 1914 Star (Clasp 2/28), the British War Medal and the Allied Victory Medal. They were received by Mrs. Magee, on behalf of her granddaughter, Kathleen Elizabeth Harrison Jankinson.

John was buried in Grave M3, Bois-Grenier Communal Cemetery, near Armentieres, Nord, France. His name is also listed on the WW1 Memorials in the Town Hall and St. Werburgh's Church, Chester.

Michael Hugh Joinson

Pte. 9th Btn. Cheshire Regiment 3751–49690

Died: 16-11-1916 age 20

Michael was the son of Michael Hugh and Elizabeth Joinson nee Norris. He was born on 29 November 1895 and baptised at St. Werburgh's on 19 January 1896. In 1909 he was also confirmed at St. Werburgh's.

Michael had one elder brother, Peter and two elder sisters and the family lived initially at Handley's Court 34 Boughton, where Michael's father carried out his joinery work. Between 1901 and 1911 Michael's father died. He was possibly the man buried in Overleigh Cemetery 1908 age 50, of 24 Steam Mill Street.

Then Michael, his sister Ellen and mother Elizabeth lived with Martin Dowd and his family at 46 Steven Street, Boughton. Martin Dowd was the husband of Michael's sister Mary. Both Martin and Michael worked for Dickson's Nurseries, Newton-by-Chester.

Michael had already served with the Territorials (first number) when he enlisted with the 3/5 Battalion of the Cheshire Regiment on 23 April 1915, giving his address now as 5 Wellington Street, Newtown, Chester and did initial training at home. On 10 February 1916 he was sent to France aboard S.S. "St. Tudno" and disembarked at Rouen the following day. On 29 February 1916 he joined his battalion in the field where he remained until 19 May when he received multiple bullet wounds in both thighs. The wounds had been treated in a field ambulance, before he was taken to 19 Casualty Clearing Station. From there he was transferred to No. 10 ambulance train and was admitted to No. 5 General Hospital, Rouen on 23 May. It was decided that he should continue his treatment at home, so he was evacuated on board SS Aberdonian, on 25 May. He remained in England, having further treatment at the Cheltenham V.A. Hospital and recuperating until 14 September 1916, when he once more set off for France.

By 9 November 1916 Michael would have been with the rest of the Battalion in the newly erected Nessin Hut camp at the village of Aveluy, Somme. The Battalion was involved in work in and around the camp until 13 November when they were ordered into the line. The Battalion was shelled on the way into the line, with 4 men killed and 6 wounded as a result, together with one officer. Enemy shelling continued day and night of 14 November. On 15th of that month, Hessian Trench was shelled during the day from Loupart Wood and Lt. W. Evans was badly injured. Enemy shelling continued during the 16 November and Lt. Evans died of his wounds. Michael Hugh Joinson also died on that same date, undoubtedly as the result of enemy shelling but it is unclear at what stage between 13 and 16 November he had been hit. Casualty losses are given in the Battalion Diary only at the end of the tour of the trenches. By 1.40am on 17 November the

Cheshires had been relieved by 7th Btn. E. Kents and the Cheshires moved into Marlborough Huts.

In 1918 his effects were sent to his mother. The commanding officer apologises that there is so little to send. The effects consisted of a religious book, a rosary in a cardboard box and some photographs.

Michael was eligible for the British War Medal and the Allied Victory Medal.

Michael's name is listed on the Thiepval Memorial, Somme, France – Pier and Face 3C and 4A. It is also listed on the WW1 Memorials in the Town Hall and in St. Werburgh's Church, Chester.

Peter Joinson

Pte. 2nd Btn. Cheshire Regiment 9291

Died: 02-03-1915 age 24

Peter was the youngest child of Peter and Elizabeth Joinson nee Jones who had married at St. John's Parish Church, Chester in 1880. Peter snr. was a blacksmith. Their family consisted of Alice who sadly died age three, Hugh Henry, Nellie, Annie and Peter jnr. Peter snr. was a Catholic and his wife Elizabeth was Anglican. All the children were baptised soon after their births, in Anglican Churches in Chester. However, Peter snr. appears to have taken at least three of the children, Henry, Annie and Peter, to St. Francis Catholic Church when they were somewhat older, also to be baptised there. St. Francis was the church where he, himself had been baptised as a baby. Peter jnr. had been baptised in St. Bridget's with St. Martin's Anglican Church on 29 October 1890 and afterwards baptised at St. Francis Catholic Church, Chester on 29 May 1896. Peter was later confirmed at St. Werburgh's in 1900.

The family appears to have lived reasonably well by the standards of the time, until 1900 when Peter snr. died aged only 39. Thereafter in the 1901 census, Elizabeth Joinson is living in Chester Workhouse with her two youngest children Annie and Peter. Henry appears to have joined the Manchester Regiment (underage) and Nellie is living with Elizabeth's sister in Hanley, Staffordshire and working as a painter of pottery. The family was able to pull through this difficult time and later Hugh Henry married Louisa Shaw in Hanley, Staffordshire in 1903. The couple set up home there. Elizabeth was received into the Catholic Church at St.Werburgh's in 1907. Later Elizabeth went to live at Vernon House in Bolton, remaining there until the end of March 1915, when she went to Hanley to live with her daughter Nellie, at 25 High Street.

Peter had joined the 3rd Battalion of the Cheshire Regiment and was sent to Special Reserve on 21 June 1908 at Chester. He was allegedly 18 years and nine months at this time and was working as a farm labourer. On 27 July 1909 he joined the regular Army with the 2nd Battalion of the Cheshires. From 23 October 1909 until 5 December 1910 he was in Belfast. On 6 December 1910 he was posted to India and stayed there until 18 November 1914. During his time there he was hospitalised twice for an illness with malaria like symptoms. His battalion then returned home and Peter was in hospital in Winchester from 4 to 8 January 1915, again with malaria.

On 16 January 1915 Peter arrived in France. Back in Chester, on 2 February 1915 Mrs. M.A. Jones (a member of Elizabeth's family) wrote from her home at Canal Side, Chester, to Peter's commanding officer, asking for news of him, because he had made no contact since he left England and the family was very worried. The worries were not unfounded. On 1 March, Nos. 2 and 3 companies took their place in the firing line trenches. On 2 March 1915 Peter was killed in action.

Peter was buried in Grave 1.A.25 of Wulverghem – Lindenhoek Road Military Cemetery, West Vlaanderen, Belgium. He had gained the 1914–15 Star, the British War Medal and the Allied Victory Medal. His mother Elizabeth, who was now living with her elder son Henry, in Hanley, Staffordshire, received these medals in 1919.

Edward Vincent Jones

Pte. Duke of Cornwall's Light Infantry 11797

Died: 12-10-1915 age 29

Edward was born in Chester on 15 June 1886, the son of John and Mary Jones, nee Higgins, both Cestrians, of Thomas Buildings, Canal Side, Boughton. He was the seventh of their nine children. Edward was baptised at St. Werburgh's on 5 July 1886 and later attended St. Werburgh's Schools. He was also confirmed there in 1899.

Edward's father John was a printing compositor and his mother Mary was a dressmaker, who worked from home. By 1901 the family had moved to 3 The Headlands, Boughton and Edward, now aged 14 was an apprentice to a coachbuilder. His two elder sisters, Elizabeth and Mary were now assistant schoolmistresses at St. Werburgh's School, having already spent several years as pupil teachers. Edward's elder brothers Ellis and Joseph were apprentices to a solicitor and on the Railway, respectively. His younger siblings Margaret and Francis were still at school. In 1909 Mary Josephine Jones married Henry Godfrey Sandfield and by 1911 only Edward and Frank were still living with their parents at their home at 10 Beaconsfield Street.

At some time between 1911 and 1914 Edward moved to London, where he was employed as a coach painter. It was here that he enlisted on 1 October 1914. He was placed first with the Northern Reserves and then later assigned to the Duke of Cornwall's Light Infantry.

Back in Chester, in 1915 due to staffing problems which were endemic during the war, Mrs. Sandfield (nee Miss M. J. Jones) was recalled to teach on supply in Standard III of St. Werburgh's Girls' Junior School. In 1916 Miss (Elizabeth) Jones is reported in the Head Mistress' Log Book as having to take both Standard V and VI, in addition to teaching singing.

On 20 May 1915 Edward embarked for France. In September of that year Edward was one of the troops who sustained a severe gas attack on Hill 60 at Ypres. His conduct on this occasion was such that he was mentioned in De Ruvigny's Roll of Honour Volume 2 Page 186. Edward was evacuated to this country and was treated in the Cornelia (Military) Hospital, Longfleet Road, Poole, Dorset where he subsequently died. On 16 October 1915, Edward's requiem mass was said at St. Mary's R.C. Church, Poole and his body was taken from the church to be buried in Poole Cemetery, grave 3.C. 2. 10038. The ceremony was conducted by Fr. Timothy Hannigan. St. Mary's Church was situated on the shore in Poole at this time. In the 1960's a new church was built further inland and the old church was used for lifeboat storage. The registers from the old church were removed to the new one.

Edward's enlistment had been reported in the March 1915 issue of St. Werburgh's Parish Magazine and his obituary was printed in the November 1915 issue. His name is listed on the WW1 Memorials in the Town Hall and St. Werburgh's Church, Chester. Edward was eligible to receive the 1914–15 Star, the British War Medal and the Allied Victory Medal.

Frederick Jones

Pte. 1st Btn. Cheshire Regiment 9619

Died: 30-10-1914 age 19 years

Frederick was the son of John and Mary Jones (nee Goulding). He was born on 2 September 1895 and baptised at St. Werburgh's on 4 September 1895. Frederick had an older sister, Margaret and a younger brother, Thomas and the family lived at 2 Steam Mill Street. Sadly their mother Mary died in May 1901 and later the family moved to 3 Mount Street, Boughton, Chester. In 1911 John Jones was living there with his two sons and working in a market garden. Frederick was working as a painter's labourer.

Frederick's enlistment papers have not survived but his number indicates that he enlisted at Chester in June/July 1913 as a regular soldier. At the outbreak of war he would have been stationed in Londonderry but went to France on 31 August 1914 when reinforcements were needed to prevent the German sweep to encompass the channel ports of the north east coast of France. He was probably one of the 78 NCOs and men from the 1st Btn. who were wounded between 15 and 22 October 1914 in action at Voilaines. He was probably treated and died at the hospital in Wimereux.

Frederick is buried in Grave 1. A. 3A. Wimereux Communal Cemetery, Pas de Calais, France. His name is listed on the WW1 Memorials in the Town Hall and in St. Werburgh's Church, Chester. Frederick was eligible to receive the 1914 Star with clasp, the British War Medal and the Allied Victory Medal.

Walter Morissey Jones

Pte. 2nd Btn. Cheshire Regiment 8768

Died: 13-02-1915 aged 23

Walter was the eldest son of Walter James and Ellen Jones nee Meacock, who were both Cestrians and from the Hoole area of the city. Ellen had been baptised at St Werburgh's in 1866 and the couple had married at St. Werburgh's on 25 November 1888. They first lived with Ellen's widowed father in Brooke Street, Walter working as a clerk. From 1902 Walter and Ellen ran the Carnarvon Castle Hotel in Watergate Street, Chester. It was on the corner of Watergate and Crook Street but is no longer used as a hotel. Walter James advertised "Bitter drawn from the wood" and "Prime Old Tenpenny Ale." In 1809 the Carnarvon Castle Hotel was used as a polling station.

Twins seemed to run in the family and their eldest child, Walter Morissey had a twin sister, Ellen Frances. They were baptised at St. Francis in 1890. His next sister was Gladys Veronica, followed by twins Austen (died young) and Winifred who were all baptised at St. Werburgh's. The youngest and allegedly most vivacious members of the family were the twin brothers, Leo and Terry who were baptised at St. Francis in January 1907. It appears to have been a very lively household. There is even a story that Terry once set a fire under the bed of his twin brother. Fortunately no permanent damage was done to either the household or family members!

After leaving school Walter Morissey trained to be an electrician. However, as soon as he reached his 18th birthday he enlisted with the Cheshire Regiment. He signed up at Chester on 9 December 1907 for a 7+5 (7years with the colours and 5 years with the reserves). He had home postings for 5 years, during which time he gained a Chiropody Certificate. He was posted to India on 18 October 1912 and was there until 18 November 1914. During his time there he was hospitalised in Jabalpur for 10 days for suspected malaria. His blood was negative for the malaria parasite on discharge but he was prescribed quinine for 4 months.

The voyage home from India, after war had been declared, took about a month and Walter was at home until 15 January 1915. From here he left for France on 16 January 1915. He was killed in action a month later, on 18 February 1915.

Walter's name is listed on the Ypres (Menin Gate) Memorial, (Panel 19–21) in West-Vlaanderen, Belgium. It is also listed on the memorials in the Town Hall and in St. Werburgh's Church, Chester. Walter was eligible to receive the 1914–15 Star, the British War Medal and the Allied Victory Medal.

Walter's father died in December 1923 but Ellen lived until 1942. They are buried in the same grave in Overleigh Cemetery, where their dead infant is also buried and their eldest son is remembered.

Patrick Kavanagh

Lce. Cpl 1st Btn. Irish Guards 10329

Died: 03-05-1918 age 36

Patrick Kavanagh was born in Liverpool, the son of Bernard Kavanagh but his parents possibly died before the Great War started. Patrick may have had a brother, James who was a baker and lived with his wife Margaret at 23 Henry Street, Chester. Perhaps he visited them and so met his future wife Elizabeth Mooney daughter of James Mooney of 30 Water Tower View, Chester. The couple were married at St. Werburgh's on 8 August 1914 and started their married life at 26 Water Tower View. Their daughter Patricia was born in May 1915 and baptised at St. Werburgh's.

Patrick enlisted with the Irish Guards at Liverpool, on 16 November 1915. At that time he and his family were living at 9 Tollemache Street in Chester and Patrick was working as a fireman. Patrick was posted to the Guards Depot. He served in this country until 16 March 1917. On 17 March he embarked at Southampton, as part of the British Expeditionary Force to France, disembarking at Le Havre the following day. On 3 July 1917 he was promoted to Lance Corporal and on 17 July sent on a signalling course at Luytpenne. On 24 August 1917, Patrick qualified as a 1st Class Signaller and received a certificate to that effect. On 28 August 1917, he was posted to field duties and on 12 September 1917 Patrick was wounded in action. He suffered shrapnel and gunshot wounds to the left hip and two days later he received a severe gunshot wound to the left thigh. This necessitated his being transported to England via "Newhaven," on 25 September 1917. Patrick received hospital treatment in this country, and must also have undertaken some course of study, because on 17 December 1917 he was awarded a third class education certificate. He remained in this country until 30 March 1918.

On 1 April 1918 Patrick re-joined the British Expeditionary Force to France, embarking at Folkstone. He disembarked at Calais the same day and re-joined his Battalion on 6 April 1918. On 5 May Patrick was wounded in action in the field. He received a gunshot wound to the head and died of this injury.

Patrick was buried in Grave I. A. 31 in Bagneux British Cemetery, Gezaincourt. He was eligible to receive the British War Medal and the Allied Victory Medal. These would have been sent to his wife Elizabeth who was then living at 19 Flinders Street, Commercial Road, Liverpool.

John Kearns

Pte. 1ˢᵗ Btn. East Yorkshire Regiment 7293

Died: 20-09-1914 age 29

John was the youngest of the five surviving children born to John and Ann Kearns nee Burke, both of whom were born in Ireland. John was born on 10 March and baptised at St. Werburgh's on 22 March, 1885. His older siblings were Mary Ann, Margaret, Patrick, and Ann. His younger sister Catherine died at less than one year old, in 1989.

The family lived at 53 Boughton and in successive censuses, John snr. and the two sons are shown as bricklayers and the girls as domestic servants. John age 26 and his sister Mary Ann age 35 are the only siblings still living at home in 1911.

Both Patrick and John were listed on St. Werburgh's Roll of Honour, drawn up for December 1914. Unfortunately, although Patrick survived to be discharged in 1917, John was already dead by the time the Roll was published.

From his army number we can deduce that John may have enlisted some time after the 1911 census and before the Great War broke out. John's enlistment papers have not survived, so we have few details of his army service but his medal roll card states that he entered France on 8 September 1914. This would indicate that John was likely to have been involved in the Battle of the Aisne, which permanently stopped the German advance upon Paris but which caused both sides to begin trench warfare.

John has no known grave but his name is recorded on the memorial in the park in La Ferte-Sous-Jouarre, 66 kilometres East of Paris. A Memorial Register is also kept at the Town Hall. In Chester it is recorded on the Town Hall Memorial Board.

James Francis Kelly

Pte. Royal Welsh Fusiliers, Royal Warwickshire Regiment 1540,
Hampshire Regiment 32035

Died: 04-11-1918 age 28

James Francis Kelly was born on 28 March 1890 and baptised on 13 April 1890 at St. Werburgh's, Chester. He was one of 6 children who were born to James and Margaret nee Hopkins. James, Margaret and all the children were born in Chester. In 1891 the family lived at Parry's Entry but by 1901 when James was 11 the family had moved to 114 Boughton. James snr. worked as a bricklayer as did his eldest son Thomas. In 1911 the family had moved to 72 Boughton where they were to remain. At that time only Thomas, John and Ann were at home. The eldest sibling Catherine was married, James was in the army and the youngest child Martin, born in 1896 had only lived 16 months.

We do not know precisely when James joined the army but he is listed on the roll of the Royal Welsh Fusiliers at Regis Barracks Wrexham, in the 1911 census. It is possible that he enlisted for a short service when he was 18. Then, when he had finished his service, he would have returned to civilian life as a Special Reservist. This would explain why he re-enlisted on 6 May 1914 at Coventry, as a Special Reservist with the 4th Btn. Royal Warwickshire Regiment, for a period of 6 years. His civilian work was stated as that of a bricklayer. He served initially in France, first entering that theatre of war on 27 May 1915.

James' time in France was fairly unremarkable for wartime but he did spend 18 days in Parkhurst hospital from 19 April to 6 May 1915, being treated for scabies. He returned to France but was in hospital at St. Omer from 23 September 1915 until 9 October 1915 suffering with influenza. At the beginning of March 1916 James was absent without leave for 3 days and received a fine as punishment. He received a shrapnel wound to his right hand on 1 July 1916 and was repatriated as the wound suppurated. He was admitted to Nerly War Hospital on 4 July, where he was first treated and Orchard Convalescent Hospital, Dartford ten days later. He remained there until 5 September 1916, when he was transferred to the Depot.

James embarked at Devonport for Salonica on 4 November 1916. This was part of an effort to re-enforce Serbian and other troops along the Macedonian front. In the spring of 1917 a great push north, against the Austro-Hungarian forces, was planned. You could say that here, on this front, the reasons for the outbreak of WW1 were crystallized, militarily. James disembarked at Salonica on 16 November 1916 but on 14 January 1917 he sustained an injury in the field. He apparently fell from an observation post in a tree and damaged his leg. James' records are difficult to decipher but it appears that he was not treated at the 82nd Field Ambulance until 25 January 1917. It was decided that full hospital treatment was needed and he was admitted to (a field) hospital on 20 February 1917. James was then taken by HMS 'Valorous' from Salonica on 27 February

1917 to Malta. Here he was admitted to hospital on 3 March 1917. The records become even more difficult to decipher from now on but it appears that James left Malta on HMS 'Ghoorka' on 9 October 1917. 'Ghoorka' was a hospital ship carrying over 300 patients and medical staff. It was damaged by a mine off Malta on 10 October. Though no-one lost their life, the ship was completely disabled and had to be towed back to Malta, where James was readmitted to hospital as a 'Ghoorka' survivor, on 20 October 1917. He left Malta for England on 1 December 1917, suffering with a malunion of fractured tibia and fibula and with dysentery and was posted to the Hampshire Regiment Depot on 11 December 1917.

James was first treated for dysentery at the General Hospital at Edgbaston in Birmingham. He left there, having tested negative for microbes, on 8 February 1918 and was transferred to the Divisional Dysentery Convalescent Hospital at Barton-on-Sea, Hants. From here he was transferred to the University War Hospital at Southampton, where his damaged right leg was treated for malunion of the tibia and fibula bones. On 21 March James returned to the second Birmingham War Hospital for more treatment on his leg. He remained there until 27 May 1918. It was here that James refused a final operation for contraction of the Achilles tendon. He was then discharged to employment.

After that James was the subject of a medical board of enquiry. The medical board was informed that James' injury was originally caused by falling from an observation post in a tree. The court heard that James had had four operations performed on his leg but that it was constantly buckling underneath his weight. His present condition was that the leg was shortened and deformed. He had also received a shrapnel-wound to his hand but this was causing no disability at that time. He had also refused an operation for contraction of the Achilles tendon. The court concluded on 28 October 1918 that James should be discharged with a pension, as he was no longer fit to carry out military duties.

James died at home in Chester on 4 November 1918, having received the last rites. He was buried from St. Werburgh's in Overleigh Cemetery on 8 November 1918 in Grave 873.

James was eligible to receive the 1914–15 Star, the British War Medal and the Allied Victory Medal. His name is on the Memorial Board in Chester Town Hall and was on the original Memorial Plaque in St. Werburgh's Church, Chester. At first it had been omitted from the plaque, because James' ailing mother had not managed to contact the church in time. The plaque was made and erected, before James' mother realised her mistake. She contacted Canon Chambers, who in turn contacted Hardman's of Birmingham, who had manufactured the plaque. Hardman's manufactured a small separate, bronze tablet, which was added to the plaque, in situ.

John Sullivan Kelly

Lce. Cpl. 1st Btn Leinster Regiment 10277

Died: 04-05-1915 age 21

John was the son of Patrick and Ann Mary Kelly, nee Swindley of Boughton, Chester, who had married at St. Werburgh's on 14 May 1890.

John was born on 2 July 1893 and baptised on 16 July 1893 at St. Werburgh's. He was also confirmed here in 1905. His elder sister, Elizabeth Mary and younger brother, Leo Joseph were also baptised here in 1892 and 1895 respectively.

From 1896 onwards John's father Patrick was no longer residing with the family. He may have died or was permanently resident in a hospital. After this the family lived in Fosbrook Street with their maternal grandfather, who was a shoemaker. Ann Mary herself worked as an upholsteress. Later she lived in Kearsland Place, Bridge Street.

In the 1911 census, John aged 17, is resident at a boarding house for working boys, in Preston. His work is listed as that of a painter. John probably stayed in Preston, because it was here that he enlisted, most likely at the beginning of the war, with the 1st Battalion Prince of Wales's Leinster Regiment.

He arrived in France on 17 March 1915 and was killed in action on 4 May 1915.

He was entitled to the 1914–15 Star, the British War Medal and the Victory Medal.

His name is on Panel 44 of the Ypres (Menin Gate) Memorial, West-Vlaanderen, Belgium. It is also listed on the memorials in the Town Hall and St. Werburgh's Church, Chester.

Philip Luke Harrington Kelly

Reg. Sgt. Major 19th Btn. Royal Welsh Fusiliers 23979

Died: 18-03-1916 age 52

Philip was born in Gibraltar ca.1864. He was the only child of Thomas Kelly and his wife Elizabeth nee Harrington. Philip's father Thomas was a musician in the Royal Navy. Philip's mother Elizabeth died soon after Philip's birth. Philip appears to have spent his early years with his Harrington relations in Portsea, near Portsmouth and later enlisted with the Royal Welsh Fusiliers at a relatively young age. His original enlistment papers have not survived. Philip married his wife Margaret in Galway on 3 February 1891. The couple moved according to Philip's military postings, with their first child Ida Frances being born in Galway, their second Margaret in Hong Kong and Lilian and Phyllis in places which are difficult to decipher on Philip's later army records. After several years service, Philip retired from the regiment and settled in Chester, becoming by 1911 the proprietor of the Red House Hotel, Dee Banks. Later he became proprietor of the Cross Foxes Hotel on the corner of Steam Mill Street and Boughton.

By the time WW1 broke out, Philip and Margaret, with their four children, Ida, Margaret, Lilian and Phyllis were well integrated into Chester society. The Cross Foxes had always provided a centre for men working in the nearby flour steam mill, lead works and railway. The Kelly family were well known locally and though the younger two members of the family were still at St. Werburgh's School in 1914, the elder two girls were at the forefront of Cestrian and St. Werburgh's Parish, life. In 1915 the annual St. Patrick's Eve Concert produced by St. Werburgh's in Chester's Music Hall, featured Ida in a tableau, (depicting Erin) and Madge (Margaret) who gave a recitation of 'Ireland's Reply to the Kaiser' and 'The Belgian Cross.' According to the Chester Chronicle of 20 March 1915, the girls were given rapturous applause. This was to be the last time that the whole family were to take part in this annual social activity.

Philip Kelly enlisted with the 13th Battalion of Royal Welsh Fusiliers, his old regiment, at Llandudno on 14 May 1915, apparently aged 48 years 6 months. There may have been some "confusion" on this occasion, about his correct age. Philip was immediately promoted to Colour Sergeant. On 11 June 1915 he was promoted to Regimental Sergeant Major and transferred to the 19th Battalion. Unfortunately he was admitted to Chester Royal Infirmary on 9 March 1916 suffering with a fistula. He died on 18 March 1916 just after that year's St. Patrick's Day festivities. Philip was buried on 23 March in Overleigh Cemetery, Fr. Hayes of St. Werburgh's officiating.

His effects and medals were sent to his wife, together with a letter of condolence from the King and Queen.

Margaret Kelly later became proprietress of the Red Lion Hotel in Tarvin. She died in 1944.

Philip Luke Harrington Kelly and his wife Margaret are buried in Grave 258 of Overleigh Cemetery, Chester.

Charles William Kennedy

Rifleman 16th Btn. Rifle Brigade (The Prince Consort's Own) P/727

Died: 03-09-1916 age 34

Charles William was the son of Michael and Jane Kennedy nee Jackson, who were married in Chester in 1872. Michael was a tailor who had been born in Ireland and Jane was a local girl. Michael had a tailor's and linen draper's shop at 129–131 Foregate. The couple eventually had 5 boys, Charles William being the fourth. He was born on 12 May 1882 and baptised at St. Werburgh's on 25 May 1882. He was also confirmed there in 1892. Charles' mother Jane died in June 1885 age 35. In the 1891 census the widowed Michael and his 5 sons are all still at home and all working in the family business.

In early 1901 Michael married Sarah Ann Roberts, from Ness and in the census later that year, Charles William is the only son still living in the parental home. By 1911 Michael had retired and his wife Sarah was running the Belgrave Hotel at 118 Foregate. In 1914 John James Kennedy, the eldest of the five brothers, was running a tailoring business from his father's former premises at 131 Foregate.

In 1908 Charles William Kennedy married Helen Margaret Dyer and the couple lived in Wandsworth, London where they brought up their young family. William worked as a clerk in the Civil Service. By the time war broke out, the couple had 3 daughters, Mary, Helen and Patricia.

Charles William enlisted at St. Pancras, Middlesex and after initial training was sent to France. As his enlistment papers did not survive little else is known of his military life. He was killed in action on 3 September 1916, presumably during military action on the Somme and was buried in Grave I.E.42 of Hamel Military Cemetery, Beaumont-Hamel, France. Pte William Kennedy was reported killed in action in the September 1916 issue of St. Werburgh's Parish Magazine.

His father Michael died later the same year and is buried in Overleigh Cemetery, Chester.

Charles William Kennedy was eligible to receive the British War Medal and the Allied Victory Medal.

Gunner Spiro Francis Kerr

Francis Spiro Kerr

Gunner A Battalion 86th Brigade Royal Field Artillery 2919, 686600

Died: 04-08-1918 age 25

Francis Spiro Kerr was the eldest child of James Francis and Anagilica Kerr nee Argyros. Anagilica had come to Liverpool, from her family home in Corfu, in order to complete her education by becoming fluent in spoken English and perfecting her other accomplishments. Whilst in this country she met James Francis Kerr and the couple were married, at St. Mary's Catholic Chapel, Warrington, on 22 November 1891.

Francis was born on 10 April and baptised on 23 April 1893, at Our Lady of Mount Carmel Church in Liverpool. The family were at that time living at 2 Vronhill Street in Liverpool, where James Francis was manager of a pawnbroker's business. Later the family moved to 172 North Hill Street and in 1900 to 70 Knowsley Road, Bootle. Each of their five children, Francis Spiro, Josephine Mary, James Leo, James Vincent and Dorothy Veronica were baptised in Our Lady of Mount Carmel or St. Patrick's Churches in Liverpool. Sadly James Leo died aged 8 months and was buried in Ford Cemetery, Liverpool.

At some time between 1905 and 1911 the family moved to 19 Beaconsfield Street, Chester, in which city James Francis was manager of another pawnbroker's firm. The family became active members of St. Werburgh's Parish. By 1911 James' son Francis had obtained a job as a clerk with a paint warehouse in Liverpool and was lodging with the Balfour family at 185 North Hill Street, Liverpool, close to one of their former homes.

On 1 December 1915 Francis Kerr enlisted with the West Lancashire Borderers of the Royal Field Artillery, giving his address as 81 Upper Stanhope Street, Liverpool. He first had a period of home service. Francis' army papers are very sparse and difficult to follow chronologically. Some information seems to be missing. However, it appears that he was sent to France on 11 April 1917. His tour of duty in France was punctuated by ill health. On 10 May 1917 Francis was admitted to the 39th Brigade's General Hospital in Le Havre. On 16 May 1917 he was posted to reinforce Le Havre. On 28 May 1917 he was posted to 86th Brigade's Field Hospital. In August 1917 his father, James Francis Kerr died in Chester and his name was published in the September issue of St. Werburgh's Parish Magazine. Francis was awarded two weeks leave in the U.K., from 12–26 January 1918, for unstated reasons. In April 1918 Francis was reported as having been missing since 21 March 1918 and later, on 4 August 1918, he was reported dead.

Some members of Francis' family have remained in the Chester area and have supplied information and a picture. He was eligible for the British War Medal and the Allied Victory

Medal. His family can remember the plaque which Francis' mother received but it is no longer in their possession.

Francis was buried in Grave VE 11 Valenciennes (St. Roch) Communal Cemetery.

James Kirby

Pte. 1ˢᵗ Btn. Royal Welsh Fusiliers 4374

Died: 25-09-1916 age 23

James was the son of Peter and Mary Kirby nee Walsh, of Parry's Entry, Foregate and later of Steam Mill Street, Chester. He was one of the five surviving children of the nine born to the family. His elder siblings were Catherine Mary, Peter and Joseph. He also had a younger brother Ernest. James was born on 13 December and baptised on 25 December 1892 at St Werburgh's.

After school James worked as an agricultural labourer. His father Peter died in1908 and on 23 August 1911 James enlisted with the Royal Welsh Fusiliers at Wrexham. He was 18 years 8 months of age and a stunning 6ft. 3 and one quarter inches height. His postings were home ones until 11 November 1914 when he was sent to France. The dates thereafter on his army service record do not strictly tally with the dates on his army medical history notes. However, what is certain is that James was posted home around the end of December 1914. On 24 May 1915 he was recorded as having deserted. On 21 June 1915 a military trial was dispensed with and he was discharged on 28 July 1915 due to the fact that injuries meant that he was physically unfit to carry out the duties of a soldier.

James' army medical board records of 6 July 1915 may help us to understand the meaning behind these bald and contradictory statements on his army record. Medical Board records state that James had been in action on 29 December 1914 at Armentieres. He had received gunshot wounds to his back and left arm and lay for nine hours before receiving medical attention. He was operated on for emphysema following double pneumonia, in hospital. The wounds on his back were healed and healthy. However, the gunshot wounds at the junction of the mid and lower thirds of the left upper arm resulted in the paralysis of the motor and sensory neurones. His hand was clawed and blue. There was atrophy of the muscles from shoulder to fingers, which showed no sign of improvement. X-rays revealed the presence of many minute foreign bodies in the arm. He was awarded a pension of 18 shillings and nine pence per week and ordered to report to another medical board on 7 June 1916. At this second medical board the police corroborated that James had received no earnings during the intervening period. Neither had his medical condition improved.

Three months after this medical board, James died. He was buried on 3 October 1916, in Overleigh Cemetery, Chester, Grave 1168, Fr. Young of St. Werburgh's officiating. His grave is under the care of the Commonwealth War Graves Commission.

James was entitled to the 1914 Star, the British War Medal and the Allied Victory Medal.

Matthew Leak

Pte. No. 3 Depot, Cheshire Regiment 5974

Died: 04-06-1920 age 42

Matthew was the youngest son of James and Ann Leak, nee Martin, of Chester. The couple had been married there in 1858. His elder siblings were Alfred, Mary Ann, Sarah Elizabeth, James, Peter, Thomas and Martha. James was a labourer and Ann was a hawker of fruit. The family lived originally at 58 Steven Street. The children were baptised at St. Werburgh's.

By 1871 the family were living at 1 Tasker's Court and by 1881 they lived at 4 Herbert's Court. In 1883 Matthew's mother died in Chester Infirmary and after that he was probably placed in Bishop Brown's Memorial Industrial School in Stockport, where he was living during the 1991 census.

On 24 November 1898 Matthew enlisted at Chester with the Cheshire Regiment, giving his age as 19 years 11 months. His address was given as 44, Boughton and it states on his papers that he had previously been refused as he was underweight. This time he was accepted for a service of 8 years. This meant that he was transferred to the Army Reserve in November 1906 but was immediately re-engaged for a period of 4 years until November 1910.

During his service Matthew had been stationed in India and South Africa. Whilst in South Africa he had gained the Queen's South Africa Medal, with clasps for Johannesburg, Orange Free State, and Cape Colony. These were all awarded in 1901, when Rings were also added to the Medal.

After being discharged from the army in November 1910 Matthew lived in a boarding house at 10 Commercial Row, Chester. His father had died in Chester, in March 1910. Matthew worked as a labourer. When the Great War broke out Matthew enlisted on 5 August 1914. He was posted immediately to the 3rd Battalion of the Cheshire Regiment, then to the 1st Battalion on 18 December 1914, when he embarked for France. Matthew did not cope well with winter trench warfare. By 8 February 1915 he had been so badly frost-bitten that he was sent to England on 10 February via "Valdivia." He was eventually sent to Chester War Hospital where, despite good nursing for a number of years, he died of complications and ensuing medical problems on 4 June 1920.

Matthew was buried in grave G1059 in Overleigh Cemetery and his grave is marked by a Commonwealth War Graves Commission headstone.

Matthew was entitled to receive the 1914–15 Star, the British War Medal and the Allied Victory Medal.

2nd Lt. Thomas Henry Lowe

Thomas Henry Lowe

2nd Lt. 7th Btn. Border Regiment

Died: 23-04-1917 age 32

Thomas was the only son of Mr. and Mrs. Henry Lowe, and was born in 1884 in Barrow-in-Furness, Lancs. His family later moved to Liverpool. Thomas entered the service of Parr's Bank in 1905, serving first at the Waterloo Branch and then in October 1911 he was transferred to Chester, Eastgate Branch. It was whilst here that he joined the congregation at St. Werburgh's and made the acquaintance of Blanche Marie Louise Genevieve Cottier.

Blanche was the eldest child of Francois Cottier, a notable French chef/restaurateur who had a business in Foregate, Chester. Her mother was Ellen nee Berry. Blanche was a music teacher, specialising in piano and an accomplished concert contralto. She acted as accompanist at the St. Patrick's Day concerts produced at the Music Hall Theatre near the Cathedral, both by St. Werburgh's and St. Francis' Parishes. She was also much in demand as a classical singer at local and northern concert halls.

In the early days of the war Thomas joined the Citizens Volunteers and then in July 1915, he was sent to the Inns of Court O.T.C. In December he was gazetted to a commission in the Border Regiment, where at first he acted as a bombing instructor at a home camp. However it was only a question of time before he would be sent overseas.

On 8 February 1917 Thomas Henry Lowe married Blanche Marie Louise Genevieve Cottier at St. Werburgh's Church, Chester. The witnesses at the marriage were Henry Raynard of 34 Newry Park, Chester and Blanche's younger sister, Doris.

Blanche continued to live at her family's home of 'Mullingar' Liverpool Road, Chester, whilst her husband Thomas took up his posting in France. He was reported missing towards the end of April. By May it was confirmed that he had been killed in action. His obituary appeared in the June 1917 issue of St. Werburgh's Parish Magazine. According to the Cheshire Observer of Saturday, 2 June, Mrs. Blanche Lowe was inundated with letters of condolence, from Buckingham Palace, the War Office and different army officers. All stressed both Lieut. Lowe's abilities as an officer and his gallantry.

Blanche's brother, Leon Louis Cottier served with the Royal Garrison Artillery during WW1 and survived this conflict to return to Chester. However, he died in 1920 and was buried in Overleigh Cemetery. Mrs. Ellen Cottier died in 1935 and her husband Francois died in Chester age 77, in 1937. Both are buried in Overleigh Cemetery in the same grave as their son, Leon.

Blanche had no child and remained a widow until her death in Runcorn in 1971 at the age of 88. Doris Cottier remained single and died in 1978, in Chester, at the age of 80.

Thomas Henry Lowe's name is listed on the Arras Memorial, Pas de Calais, France, Bay 6. In Chester his name is on the Memorial Board in the Town Hall, in the National Westminster Bank at 33 Eastgate (formerly Parrs Bank) and that in St. Werburgh's Church. He was entitled to the British War Medal and the Allied Victory Medal.

John Ludden

Pioneer 9ᵗʰ Labour Company, Royal Engineers 122804

Died: 15-05-1916 age 46

John was the son of Thomas and Bridget Ludden nee Nyland of Newport, Shropshire. John was born there in 1870, the eldest of a family of nine siblings, Mary, Ellen, Thomas, Daniel, Patrick, Martin, Bridget and Catherine. Sadly Bridget died soon after her birth.

In 1893 John's mother Bridget died, followed by sister Mary and Patrick's wife Catherine in 1897. Catherine left a small son, Daniel. Some time after this, John and his younger brother Thomas moved to Chester. This could have been because there was another Ludden family living in Chester at the time, to which John's family may have been related.

John worked as a bricklayer, boarding with many similarly employed men at a lodging house at 17 Claremont Walk, Boughton. Thomas was a fish seller and boarded at the Elephant and Castle in Northgate Street. Their younger brother Martin died in 1901 age 19 and their father died in 1903, both in Newport, Shropshire. After this, the other two brothers, Patrick and Daniel with their sister Catherine also moved to Chester, presumably bringing Patrick's son, Daniel with them. Their sister Ellen had married in Newport in 1902. Thomas Ludden married Mary Walsh at St. Werburgh's Chester in October 1904 and was at that time living in Princess Street, Chester. Later in that same year, his brother Patrick died and was buried in Overleigh Cemetery. His sister Catherine married Patrick Kelly at St. Werburgh's in 1910.

In 1902 John had married Catherine Hunt in Oldham. The family then lived at 47 Derwent Street, Oldham and in the 1911 census the couple had four children, Thomas, Catherine, Mary and Ellen. In 1913 their son John was born. The family may also have had some care for Daniel, John's orphaned nephew, who was an apprentice baker in Oldham.

John's enlistment papers have not survived, so there are few details of his military service. However on his Medal Roll Card it states that he served in France from 2 October 1915, indicating that he probably enlisted in the latter part of 1914 or early in 1915. He served there until his death from wounds on 15 May 1916. Pte John Ludden was reported killed in action in the June 1916 issue of St. Werburgh's Parish Magazine. His effects were sent to his wife Catherine, at 14 Woolscott Street, Oldham.

John is buried in Grave VIII A 110 in the Eastern Part of Boulogne Cemetery.

He was entitled to receive the 1914–15 Star, British War Medal and the Allied Victory Medal.

Owen McCleary

Pte.Welsh Regiment 27228

Died: 08-08-1915 age 28 years

Owen was the son of Christopher and Julia McCleary nee Flynn, who married in Manchester in 1868. Christopher had been born in County Mayo but lived in Dublin with his three brothers for a short while, before coming to England. One brother settled in Manchester, two in Chester and the fourth in an unknown town. Christopher and the brother who also settled in Chester, were tailors.

Christopher and Julia set up house in the Boughton area of Chester and brought up their family of eleven children there. Owen was born in 1887 and was baptised, as all his siblings had been, in St. Werburgh's Church, shortly after. He was also confirmed there in 1899. All the McCleary siblings attended St. Werburgh's Schools. In 1891 the family lived at 12 Steam Mill Street but by 1901 they had moved to number 1. In 1911 they were at 3 Fosbrook Street.

Owen's enlistment papers have not survived but his medal roll card has. This implies that he had enlisted in 1914. He took part in the Balkans campaign, first entering the theatre of conflict on 4 July 1915. One month later he was missing presumed dead at Gallipoli. Six months later he would have been officially registered as such.

Owen was buried at Gallipoli, Carakkale, Turkey and is named on the Helles Memorial. He was entitled to the 1914–15 Star, the British War Medal and the Allied Victory Medal. Owen's name is also on the Town Hall memorial, Chester though his regiment is incorrectly named.

James McCormack

Pte. 1st Btn. King's Own Royal Lancaster Regiment 7505

Died: 29-10-1914 age 33

James was the eldest child of Patrick and Elizabeth McCormack nee Kendrick, born on 2 October 1881 and baptised 9 October at St. Werburgh's. Patrick had been born in Ireland and Elizabeth in Buckley. They lived at 117 Christleton Road and later at Watkins Court in Pitt Street. In 1901 James, his father and his younger brother Edward were working as nurserymen and gardeners in Chester. James also had other younger siblings Annie, Charles, Thomas, Rose, Elizabeth and Helen. Sometime after this census was taken, Patrick died and James decided to join the army.

James enlisted first with the 1st Cheshires at Frodsham, on 18 September 1902 aged 20 years. He was transferred almost immediately to the K.O.R. Lancaster Regiment. He was trained and had postings at home until 9 February 1904, when he was then posted to Lucknow, India. He returned home 18 January 1905 and remained in this country until his second posting to India on 14 February 1906. He was to be in India for four years until 26 June 1910. After a stint at home he was sent to France on 27 October 1914. Two days later, James was struck by gunfire and sustained abdominal wounds. He was treated at 06 Field Ambulance XI and later admitted to hospital where he died of his wounds. On 30 October 1914 he was buried in the temporary Cemetery of La Meuve, Bi Bon Jean. The death of Pte. James McCormack was reported in the December 1914 issue of St. Werburgh's Parish Magazine.

In April 1915 Elizabeth McCormack received a letter from Infantry Offices asking for her correct address to which her son's medals and other effects could be sent. In 1921 she eventually received her son's British War Medal, Allied Victory Medal, and 1914 Star with clasp, at her home in Tarvin Workhouse. She died later that year.

James is buried in Grave IX.A.24 Cite Bonjean Military Cemetery, Armentieres, Nord, France.

Patrick A. McDonald

Pte. 4th Btn. Grenadier Guards 25051

Died: 27-09-1916 age 36

Patrick was born in Westport Co. Mayo but must have moved later, presumably with his family, to Chester. In 1901 he was lodging with the Jennings family of 11 Steven Street and working as a labourer in a market garden. In 1904 he married Margaret Jennings, in St. Werburgh's and the following year their son John was born and baptised there. In the 1911 census Patrick and his family are living at 16 Steven Street and Patrick is working as a construction labourer age 34. As you can see there is some confusion in official data as to what is Patrick's correct date of birth.

Patrick enlisted in Chester on 9 December 1915, his age stated as 35 years and eight months. He served at home until 12 August 1916. The following day he was posted with the British Expeditionary Force to France. He died there, from wounds received, on 27 September 1916. His wife, Margaret was notified on 22 November 1916 and she was awarded a widow's pension of 18/9d per week, on 28 May 1917.

Pte. Patrick McDonald was reported killed in action in the December 1916 issue of St. Werburgh's Parish Magazine. He was entitled to receive the British War Medal and the Allied Victory Medal.

He is buried in Grave IV.I.53, Heilly Station Cemetery, Mericout-L'Abbe, Somme, France.

James McElmeel

Pte. The King's (Liverpool Regiment) 94672

Died: 24-02-1919 age 19

James was the son of Patrick and Ellen McElmeel of 17 Seaville Street, Chester. Patrick was a bricklayer. By 1911 the couple had been married for 21 years and ten children had been born to them, five of whom had died in infancy. The surviving children were Thomas, John, James, Felix and Elizabeth Rose. James was born on 25 November 1899 and baptised at St. Werburgh's on 3 December that same year. James was also confirmed at St. Werburgh's in 1910.

After war broke out it seems that Thomas, John and James enlisted. Because of his age, James' enlistment would have been towards the end of the war and his papers have not survived, so we have little direct information about his army career. James also has no medal roll card, which indicates that he was not sent abroad. He would actually have been too young to be so sent. At this time his parents were living at 13 Steam Mill Street, Chester.

James died in this country and was buried in Overleigh Cemetery Grave 1186. His grave is marked by a Commonwealth War Graves Commission headstone.

Thomas Patrick McElmeel

Sgt. 20th Btn. Manchester Regiment 25924

Died: 04-10-1918 age 26

Thomas was the son of Patrick and Ellen McElmeel of 17 Seaville Street, Chester. Patrick was a bricklayer. By 1911 the couple had been married for 21 years and ten children had been born to them, five of whom had died in infancy. The surviving children were Thomas, John, James, Felix and Elizabeth Rose. Thomas, John and Felix were confirmed at St. Werburgh's in 1905.

After war broke out Thomas, John and James enlisted. Thomas enlisted with the 27th Reserve Battalion of the Manchester Regiment on 18 November 1915, age 23, at Prees Heath. His army career progressed very smoothly. He was appointed Lance Corporal on 3 February 1916, Corporal on 23 June 1916, Lance Serjeant on 10 July 1916 and Serjeant on 22 August 1916. Thomas spent the first year in training at home. He was in France from January 1917 until October 1918, with spells of leave from the front.

Thomas was killed in action on 4 October 1918 and was buried in Beaurevoir Communal Cemetery, British Extension, Grave B6. His younger brother John survived the war but James died. Felix was too young to enlist. Thomas' father Patrick received his British War Medal and Allied Victory Medal, after the end of the Great War. Thomas' name is listed on the Great War Memorial Board in Chester Town Hall.

John McGetrick

Gunner 168th Siege Bty. Royal Garrison Artillery 284995

Died: 21-10-1918 age 36

John, with his younger sister Mary Ellen (Nellie), was one of the two surviving children of Thomas and Rose McGetrick nee McLoughlin, both of whom had been born in Chester. Eleven other siblings had died in infancy. John was born on 7 January and baptised on 22 January 1882, at St. Werburgh's, where his father had also been baptised. The family lived at 10 Love Street and later at Canal Side. From 1901 until 1905 John served with the Royal Garrison Artillery, No. 9995. He was discharged in June 1905 after four years, as he was deemed medically unfit to work out the remainder of his service.

On 1 November 1910 John married Mary Serdiville at St. Francis, Chester and the couple lived at 19 Suffolk Street. At that time John worked as an asylum attendant in Chester. Later the couple moved to 27 Cornwall Street. Their son, John Vincent was born on 19 July 1913 and baptised on 21 August 1913 at St. Werburgh's. Sadly John Vincent died in March 1914 and was buried on 2 April in Overleigh Cemetery. After this, John and Mary moved to Westbury-on-Severn, Gloucestershire where John worked as a male nurse at the asylum in Westbury. The couple lived in one of the cottages on the asylum estate. It is not clear whether John had moved voluntarily, or whether he was redirected due to war conditions.

On 13 September 1916 John had an army medical at Harfield Barr, Bristol. It was noted that he had been previously discharged from the army due to ill health but that this was not sufficiently severe now, as to cause his rejection from service. John enlisted on 22 January 1917 and was posted immediately to the depot of his former unit, the Royal Garrison Artillery. He had several postings to different R.G.A. Depot in this country, including Catterick. Though his army papers are difficult to decipher it appears that John was posted in early 1918 to France. He experienced an intense gas attack in October 1918 and was taken to No. 9 General Hospital in Rouen. Here he died on 21 October 1918 from a mixture of the effects of gas and influenza. John was buried in Grave S.II.R.6 of St. Severin Cemetery Extension, Rouen.

His effects which consisted of letters, 2 crucifixes, a silver watch and strap, key, rosary, 3 badges, gold shell ring with stone metal ring, purse, 2 wallets, coins, photos and cards, were forwarded to his wife Mary, at the asylum cottages at Westbury-on-Severn. In 1922, his next of kin, for purposes of receiving medals, apart from his wife, included his parents who were now living at 4 Love Street and his sister Mrs. Nellie Davis, living at Wellington Street, Chester. John was entitled to receive the British War Medal and the Allied Victory Medal.

John Strain McGrogan

Bmdr. Calcutta Volunteer Artillery Bty. of the Indian Army, Royal Field Artillery

Died: 07-01-1917 age 27

John was the elder child and only son of John Sinclair McGrogan and his wife Minnie nee Anderson, who had married in 1888. He had a younger sister Wilhelmina Govanloch McGrogan. John snr. was a tailor's cutter and moved from town to town plying his trade. The two children were born in Queensferry, Linlithgowshire, Scotland, John in 1890 and Wilhelmina two years later. In 1901 the family was living at 2 Eyre Terrace, Edinburgh but by 1911 the family were at 108 Lowther Street, Penrith. Interestingly John jnr. age 21 is missing from this family entry in the census. He is listed separately as a lodger, with John and Ellen Buckingham at 199 Great Cheetham Street, Manchester and working as a tailor's cutter like his father.

The next official appearance of John Strain McGrogan is in the records of the Peninsular and Orient Shipping and Naval Company, where he is listed as a passenger on the "Borneo" travelling to Calcutta. He had sailed from London on 19 July 1913. The ship's documents do not state his reasons for travel, so we can only assume that John was seeking adventure and was going to ply his trade in India. Presumably he did just that, until his life was turned up side down by the Great War. John appears to have enlisted immediately with the Calcutta Volunteer Artillery of the Indian Army. At some stage he transferred to the Royal Field Artillery and was later taken prisoner of war by the Turks.

The exact date and place of his capture is not recorded, so we can only speculate that it was connected with the Gallipoli campaign. Likewise we have no idea of how long his incarceration lasted. We only know that John Strain McGrogan died of dysentery in a Turkish Prisoner of War camp on 7 January 1917. The contact address of his parents at this time was 14 Station Road, Padiham, Burnley.

Another mystery about John Strain McGrogan is that we have no idea how his name came to be listed on our original Great War Memorial Plaque. We can only surmise that he lived for a short time in Chester, most likely between April 1911 and July 1913 when he left for Calcutta. He may have come to Chester on his own or perhaps with his parents. His parents, if they lived here, had obviously moved to Padiham by the time that John had enlisted. Later still they moved back to Penrith in Cumbria.

The November 1917 issue of St. Werburgh's Parish Magazine stated that John Strain McGrogan had died as a Prisoner of War in Turkey. His name is listed on the Angora Memorial 110, Baghdad (North Gate) War Cemetery, on the special Kipling Memorial. It was to this cemetery that bodies of soldiers who had been buried in cemeteries in Anatolia, Turkey were brought for reburial.

John's name is also listed on the memorial in St. Catherine's Catholic Church, Penrith near where his parents and sister remained for the rest of their lives. John Strain McGrogan was entitled to the 1914–15 Star, the British War Medal and the Allied Victory Medal.

Maurice Joseph Morahan

Pte. 1st/4th Btn. "A" Company Cheshire Regiment 50311

Died: 07-10-1918 age 32

Maurice Joseph Morahan was the sixth of ten children born to William and Honoria (Norah) Morahan of Clonmore, Piltown, County Kilkenny, Ireland. We know little about his early life but he must have come to Chester looking for work or adventure some time between 1901 and 1914.

In 1914 he was living at 20 Philip Street in Hoole and it was from here that he enlisted with the Cheshire Regiment on 22 September 1914, age 28 years and 9 months. He was based for much of his early service at the Infantry Base Depot where he joined the 16th Battalion of the Cheshires. His service was scattered with odd few days treatment for scabies in Military Hospitals in Yarmouth and Bedford and disciplinary forfeits for overstaying leave in June 1915 or not returning to billet before 9.30 pm.

On 19 January 1917 Maurice disembarked at Rouen and he spent the rest of his army service in France and Flanders. On 9 February 1918 he was attached to 178 Tunnelling Company of the Royal Engineers. On 26 April he was wounded and treated at the Infantry Base Depot. Leave in U.K. was granted from 20 June to 4 July 1918. Maurice was then posted to the 1st/4th Battalion of the Cheshires. He was killed in action on 7 October 1918.

In 1919 his effects were sent to his mother in Ireland. Norah Morahan sent a letter back, thanking the army authorities for forwarding her son's effects and sorrowfully asking that if any other effects were found later, she would be very glad if they could be sent to her. In 1920 Maurice's British War Medal and Allied Victory Medal were sent to his father, William.

Maurice is buried in Grave I.D.20 of Zantvoorde British Cemetery, Belgium.

Benjamin Morley

Lce. Cpl. 1ˢᵗ Btn. Somerset Light Infantry 44538, previously 13090 Shropshire Light Infantry

Died: 24-10-1918 age 35

Benjamin was born in Buckley, Flintshire, Wales on 1 March 1883. He was the son of James and Jane Morley nee Parry, had elder brothers Joseph, Frederick and William, a younger brother Walter and younger sister Emma. By 1891 the family were living at Sandycroft Cottages in Hawarden, where James and his two elder sons were working as bricklayers. The rest of the children were still at school. By 1901 the family had moved to 81 Philip Street in Hoole, Chester but only Benjamin and his two younger siblings were still living at home. James was working as a bricklayer and Benjamin and Walter were working as council road labourers.

In 1902 Benjamin married Margaret Byrne in Chester and they set up home at 10 Henry Street, Hoole. Their children Benjamin, Frank, Eleanora, Walter and Bernard were all born there and all were baptised at St. Werburgh's. Benjamin himself had been received into the Catholic Church in December 1902 at St. Werburgh's and confirmed there in May 1905. By 1911 the family were living at 72 Trafford Street and this was the address given when Eleanora (Norah) started at St. Werburgh's Girls' School in 1914. When Bernard started at St. Werburgh's Boys' School the family was living at 37 Trafford Street.

When war broke out Benjamin enlisted with the 8ᵗʰ Battalion Shropshire Light Infantry. His name was placed on the Roll of Honour in St. Werburgh's Parish Magazine in December 1914. After training he was sent to France on 5 September 1915. Later he was transferred to the 1ˢᵗ Battalion Somerset Light Infantry. Having survived most of the conflict he was killed in action on 24 October 1918, shortly before the Armistice.

Benjamin was buried in Grave A.11 of Verchain British Cemetery, Verchain-Maugre, France. His name was recorded on the Great War Memorial Board in Chester Town Hall. Benjamin was entitled to receive the 1914–15 Star, the British War Medal and the Allied Victory Medal.

Benjamin and Margaret's children, Frank and Norah were married at St. Werburgh's in 1929 and 1930 respectively.

Private Alfred Mullins

Alfred Mullins

Pte. 1/5th Btn. Cheshire Regiment 50560

Died: 14-04-1917 age 19

Alfred was the son of John and Ann Mullins nee Moran of 19 William Street, Chester. His father had been born in Halifax, Nova Scotia and his mother was born in Chester. They were married at St. Werburgh's on 20 February 1897. Alfred was the eldest of their five children, his siblings being Constance, Winifred, John and Ann. All the children were born in Chester, all were baptised at St. Werburgh's and all of them attended St. Werburgh's Schools. Sadly Constance died age 3, in 1902. Alfred was confirmed here in 1909, later became a member of St. Werburgh's Club and was an active worker in the affairs of the church.

In 1911 Alfred was an apprentice joiner with the McPhelan Brothers Builders on Cow Lane Bridge. Alfred enlisted on 10 December 1915, first joining the 4th reserve Battalion of the Cheshire Regiment. On 4 July 1916 he was transferred to the 1/5th Battalion. On 9 February 1917 he was posted to the British Expeditionary Force to go to France, disembarking at Rouen on 11 February 1917. Here he joined the 1st Battalion on 27th of that same month. Alfred's conduct during military engagements was such that his name was listed in the De Ruvigny Roll of Honour. He was killed in action on 14 April 1917. Pte Alfred Mullins was reported dead in the June 1917 issue of St. Werburgh's Parish Magazine.

Alfred's name is listed on the Arras Memorial, Faubourg D'Amiens Cemetery, Pas de Calais, France – Bay 5 and 6. In Chester his name is listed on the WW1 memorials in the Town Hall and in St. Werburgh's Church. He was entitled to the British War Medal and the Allied Victory Medal.

Driver Joseph Murphy

Joseph Murphy

Driver 1ˢᵗ Company, Army Service Corps, Catterick TS/268A

Died: 21-11-1916 age 40/46/55

Joseph was born in Ballingarry, Limerick. His wife Mary Bridget was born in Limerick City. The couple were married in Dublin on 2 April 1896. Joseph had previously been married to Mary's sister and they had an infant son, also called Joseph. Joseph jnr.'s mother had died soon after his birth. Mary married Joseph snr. to prevent the child, her nephew, being taken into care. Joseph had served a seven year apprenticeship as a tailor with Messrs. Brothers and by 1902 the family had moved to Cork City, where the two eldest of their surviving children Albert George and Victoria Bridget were born. Later they moved to Liverpool, where May Margaret was born in 1907. In the 1911 census the family lives at 46a Haigh Street, Liverpool. Both Joseph and Mary record their ages as 39 years. Joseph jnr. is no longer living at home.

Sometime between 1911 and 1914 the family moved to Chester, where Joseph was employed by Messrs. Delany of Northgate Street. They lived at 36 St. James' Street and joined the congregation at St. Werburgh's Church.

At the outbreak of war Joseph enlisted immediately in Chester, for the duration of the war, giving his age as 38 years. He spent most of his military service stationed at Catterick Camp, in North Yorkshire. He was able to get weekend leave from time to time and so was able to visit his family in Chester. The Chester Observer of Saturday, 7 December 1916 which gives Joseph's age as 46, also states that his son Joseph enlisted at the beginning of the war, with the East Lancashire Regiment and served throughout the Dardanelles campaign.

On the night of Saturday, 18 November Joseph was walking along the road back to camp. Near the camp he was knocked down by a car. Joseph, concussed and bleeding, was taken to the camp hospital, where he never regained consciousness. His next of kin was stated as being present at his death on the following Tuesday. He was laid to rest on the following Saturday, in Catterick Cemetery, Grave BB6, with full military honours. Wreaths were sent by officers, N.C.O's and privates of his company.

The army medical officer reported that the symptoms displayed by Joseph during his last days indicated that he had suffered laceration of the brain. He also noted that Joseph appeared older than his attested age and was in his opinion at least 55 years old.

An inquest held on 7 November 1916 decided that the death had been due to a tragic accident and later his widow was awarded 15 shillings per week for the duration of the war and 12 months thereafter.

Joseph would not have been entitled to receive any military campaign medals, as he did not take part in any campaigns abroad. His grave is however marked and maintained by the Commonwealth War Graves Commission.

It is unusual, though not unheard of, in the annals of St. Werburgh's, to have two generations, father and son, on active service during the Great War. It is unusual, however, for them both to have the same name. The opportunities for confusion are multiple.

The family of Joseph Murphy remained in Chester and Joseph's daughter May was educated at St. Werburgh's Schools, until the age of fourteen. Her elder sister, Victoria married Leonard Kilbank at St. Werburgh's in 1925. The couple later moved to Lancashire.

Reproduced by kind permission of the Commonwealth War Graves Commision.

Maurice Murphy

Pte. 2nd/9th Btn. Manchester Regiment 352363

Died: 09-10-1917 age 20

Maurice was the younger son of John Murphy and his wife Ellen nee Kennedy, both of Crook Street, who were married on 9 November 1893 at St. Francis' in Chester. John had been born in Ireland and Ellen was born in Burslem, Staffordshire. John worked as a nursery gardener and the family lived at 7 Claremont Walk, Chester. They had two sons, Michael born in 1896 and Maurice born 25 August and baptised 12 September 1897 at St. Francis'. Sadly Ellen died in 1903 and on 3 March 1908 John married Mary Byrne at St. Francis' in Chester.

By 1911 the family had moved to 1 Edward's Court, Princess Street and Michael had left St. Werburgh's School to work as an assistant to a hairdresser. Maurice was still at St. Werburgh's School. Both brothers were confirmed at St. Werburgh's Church in 1912. Maurice left school at about this time and started work at the Co-op store on George Street in Chester.

Maurice's enlistment papers have not survived, so it is difficult to uncover any details of his military service. However we do know from Chester Chronicle reports that all three male members of the Murphy family, father and both sons, were on active service abroad during the Great War. Maurice's medal roll card indicates that he probably enlisted in 1915 or 1916 and died during the second Battle of the Somme, often referred to as Passchendaele. He is buried in Grave IX. E. 1 Maurice was entitled to receive the British War Medal and the Allied Victory Medal. His name is on the Memorial Board in the Town Hall, Chester.

John O'Hara

Pte.

Died: 1916

There is some confusion about the possible identity of the man listed on our memorial board, who had been reported killed in action in the October 1916 issue of St. Werburgh's Parish Magazine.

He is possibly the son of Francis O'Hara (son of Cornelius) and Agnes O'Connor, married 13 May 1896. John O'Hara was born in 1897. This would make him 19 years old when he died.

James and Winifred O'Hara nee Armstrong were also members of the parish, living at 112 Boughton. They had children Mary Kathleen 1910, James Joseph 1911, Winifred Rose 1913, Eileen 1914, all of whom attended St. Werburgh's Schools. Mary, the child who entered in 1915 had her next of kin stated as James O'Hara and address as 110 Boughton. Subsequent children have their next of kin stated as Winefride O'Hara, with the same address. Perhaps it should be James O'Hara on the memorial board, not John.

John O'Hara, godfather to Mary Kathleen on 27 March 1910, eldest child of James and Winifred, could be the brother of James and the man listed on St. Werburgh's Memorial.

James O'Hara has a brother John who lives in Liverpool. He married a Liverpool girl Ann in 1910 and they had a son James in 1911. John was aged 25 in the 1911 census and he could also be the person who died.

The Commonwealth War Graves Commission gives John O'Hara son of James and Catherine of Annaghmore, Kilfree, Sligo, Ireland. James O'Hara of Chester was born in the same place.

Patrick O'Leary

This name was on the original memorial in St. Werburgh's, but not on the Town Hall Memorial, nor St Francis. There does not appear to be an O'Leary family who are parishioners of St. Werburgh's around this time. The possibilities from Commonwealth War Graves Commission records are as follows:

O'LEARY, PATRICK

Rank: Private

Service No: 3207

Date of Death: 24/09/1916

Age: 25

Regiment/Service: King's Own Yorkshire Light Infantry,1st/4th Btn.

Grave Reference: XI. A. 14A.

Cemetery: ETAPLES MILITARY CEMETERY

Additional Information: Son of Michael and Johanna O'Leary, of Ballybeg, Farranfore, Co. Kerry.

O'LEARY, PATRICK

Rank: Private

Service No: 21466

Date of Death: 28/06/1916

Age: 40

Regiment/Service: Lancashire Fusiliers, 1st Btn.

Grave Reference: II. B. 17.

Cemetery: AUCHONVILLERS MILITARY CEMETERY

Additional Information: Son of Michael and Ellen O'Leary, of Kilmanor, Ireland; husband of Bridget O'Leary, of 296 Tarrent Terrace, Godregraig, Glam. Born at Rawalpindi, India.

O'LEARY, JOHN PATRICK

Rank: Private

Service No: 11180

Date of Death: 17/08/1916

Age: 37

Regiment/Service: Duke of Cornwall's Light Infantry, "C" Coy. 7th Btn.

Grave Reference: Near North-West corner.

Cemetery: MONDICOURT COMMUNAL CEMETERY

Additional Information: Husband of Eleanor O'Leary, of 80 "C" Block, Guinness Buildings, Vauxhall, London.

O'LEARY, ROBERT PATRICK

Rank: Private

Service No: 13655

Date of Death: 02/10/1918

Age: 24

Regiment/Service: The Loyal North Lancashire Regiment, 1st Btn.

Panel Reference: Panel 7.

Memorial: VIS-EN-ARTOIS MEMORIAL

Additional Information: Son of Michael and Anastasia O'Leary, of 5 Chaucer Place, Liverpool.

There is no way of knowing which, if any, of these men was the one whose name was inscribed on the original St. Werburgh's Great War Memorial Plaque.

Michael Patterson

Pte. 2nd Btn. Cheshire Regiment 10324

Died: 16-04-1915 age about 39

Michael was born in Chester, the son of David and Mary Ann Patterson nee Carlin of Foregate. He first joined the Cheshire Regiment in 1895 aged nearly 19 years. He served for 16 years, seeing 3½ years service in India, until in 1911 he was discharged to the Special Reserves.

In 1911 he married Mary Eileen Campbell at St. Werburgh's and their daughter Mary Eileen was born the following year. She was baptised on 12 January 1913 at St. Francis, as the family were then living in Knights Court, Beaver Street, Chester.

When WW1 broke out Michael re-enlisted with the Cheshires, at Stockton-on-Tees, for one year's service with the Special Reserve. Michael arrived in France, 11 March 1915 and the 2nd Battalion were billeted at Vlamertinghe from 12 April. On 15 April at 5.00 pm the Battalion proceeded to Zonebeeke via Ypres, to relieve the 8th Battalion Middlesex Regiment in trenches. By 2.00 am on 16 April the trench relief was completed, with the Battalion occupying the Right Sector of Brigade line, named A Sector 1-2-3. By 12 noon 2 other ranks had been killed and 3 wounded. Michael could have been one of the two killed.

Michael Patterson was reported killed in action in the June 1915 edition of St. Werburgh's Parish Magazine. Michael's wife had died in 1918 and so Michael's seven year old daughter Mary Eileen received her father's plaque, memorial scroll and message from the King, in 1919. Later she also received his 1914–15 Star, British War Medal and Allied Victory Medal. Miss Mary Eileen Patterson was living with her maternal grandmother, Mrs. Edith Gough of 27 Seaville Street, Boughton, Chester at this time.

Michael Patterson's name is recorded on the Ypres (Menin Gate) Memorial, West-Vlaanderen, Belgium- Panel 19–22. In Chester it is written on the WW1 memorials in the Town Hall and in St. Werburgh's Church.

John Hatton Peet

Pte. Royal Fusiliers, posted to 2nd/2nd Btn.
London Regiment (Royal Fusiliers) 167478

Died: 26-10-1917 age 26

John was born in mid 1891, a middle son of Henry and Mary Ellen Hatton Peet nee Turner. John had ten siblings. He was born in Warrington but was brought up in St. Helens, where his father had a successful butcher's business. By 1911 Henry had retired and John was running the family business.

Little is known of John's army life, as his enlistment papers have not survived. His medal roll card indicates that he started his army career as a member of the Army Service Corps. Then, at some later stage he was transferred to the 2nd Battalion London Regiment of the Royal Fusiliers.

John's name is listed on the Tyne Cot Memorial, West-Vlaanderen, Belgium – Panel 28–30 and 162–162A and 163A.

In 1925 John's brother, Henry Hatton Peet married Ann Mary Thomas in St. Werburgh's Church. In 1928 Henry and John's mother, Mary Ellen died. Henry Hatton Peet endowed a rosary window in St. Werburgh's to the memory of his brother John and mother Mary Ellen. St. Werburgh's WW1 Memorial is the only one in Chester where John Hatton Peet's name is listed.

Albert Henry Pickering

Gunner 6th Siege Bty. Royal Garrison Artillery 24398

Died: 22-07-1915 age 36

Albert was born in Co. Durham the son of Thomas and Mary Pickering. He had elder siblings William, Thomas, Anne, Elizabeth, Frederick and Isobel and a younger brother Joseph. The family moved around the northern part of England, presumably following the work available to Albert's father. In the 1891 census his father is employed in the iron works at Redcar and Albert is still at school, though aged 15 years. As normal school leaving age was 13, this suggests that Albert may have been receiving what was referred to as "secondary education." In 1913 Albert married Teresa Gibbin, in Middlesborough and in late 1914 their daughter Kathleen was born.

Albert must have enlisted immediately war broke out because his medal roll card states that he entered a theatre of war (presumably France and Belgium) on 25 September 1914. According to the report in the Chester Chronicle of 24 July 1915 Albert had been wounded on New Year's Day. He was later transferred to Chester Royal Infirmary suffering from blood poisoning set up by his wound. According to the records at St. Francis' Church, Chester he died on 20 July 1915 having been given the last rites. He was buried on 24 July in Grave 4060 of Overleigh Cemetery.

Albert was entitled to receive the 1914 Star, the British War Medal and the Allied Victory Medal. His name is on the War Memorial in St. Peter's Church, Redcar.

George Price

Driver Army Service Corps DM2/164787

Died: 03-05-1917

We know little about George Price, who was received into the Catholic Church at St. Werburgh's on 24 April 1916 age 20. His parents are not named on his conditional baptism entry, nor are his army records available. Therefore we can only guess which Chester family he belonged to.

The most likely family seems to be that of Thomas and Mary Price, who lived at 46 Granville Road, in 1911. Thomas was a joiner. Their family consisted of Emma, Ivy, George (age 16) Harold, Doris and Gladys.

George attested with the Signal Company of the Royal Engineers but later transferred to the Army Service Corps. His enlistment papers have not survived so we know little of his army career. George died in May 1917, probably during the Arras Offensive of April-May of that year. Some time after this date, Fr. Maurice Hayes wrote R.I.P. against his conditional baptism entry.

George was entitled to receive the British War Medal and the Allied Victory Medal. His name is on the Arras Memorial, Bay 10.

John Rafferty

Pte. 1ˢᵗ/5ᵗʰ Btn. Cheshire Regiment 241037, previously 3480 Infantry Base Depot

Died: 19-04-1917 age 34

John was born in 1883 in Chester, the son of Thomas and Mary Rafferty. Thomas was a general labourer. John had two older brothers and a sister, Thomas, James, and Mary. He also had a younger brother Henry. In 1901 the family lived at 2 Bateman's Court, Foregate, Boughton, when John age 17 was working as a seed shop porter. This was probably at Dicksons Seeds in Eastgate, Chester. James Rafferty enlisted with the A.S.C. in 1903, where his profession was stated as a groom.

In 1908 John's father Thomas died and also John married Sarah Ann Murray of St. Helens. By 1911 John was working as a market gardener, probably for Dicksons Seeds in Newton-by-Chester. The couple lived at Greenock Place, Crook Street, Chester and had two children Margarite age 2 and John, 3 months old. Both children had been baptised at St. Francis' Chester. Sadly the baby John died before his first birthday.

Brothers Thomas and Henry lived with Mary Rafferty snr., now a widow, at 8 Victoria Buildings, Lower Bridge Street, Chester. John's sister Mary had married Mark Walsh at St. Werburgh's in 1910. Meanwhile, their brother James' health had deteriorated and he died in 1913 at the Old Sarum Workhouse Infirmary. Death was due to endocarditis and double mitral disease.

John's army papers have not survived, so it is difficult to detail his army career. As he was previously at the Infantry Base Depot, it is possible that he was called up soon after war was declared. John died on 19 April 1917, during the spring offensive and his name is listed on the Arras Memorial, Bay 5 and 6. He was eligible to receive the British War Medal and the Allied Victory Medal.

In Loving Memory
of

LIEUTENANT PETER JOSEPH RAHILL
CHESHIRE REGIMENT ATTACHED R.A.F.,
BORN JUNE 19TH 1897.
KILLED AT WINCHESTER JUNE 2ND 1918.
R.I.P.

ALSO CAPTAIN JAMES RAHILL,
LATE OF THE ROYAL IRISH FUSILIERS,
AND THE HYTHE SCHOOL OF MUSKETRY.
FATHER OF THE ABOVE
BORN 29TH JULY 1869. DIED 8TH MAY 1944.

Peter Joseph Rahill

Lieutenant 5th Btn. Cheshire Regiment, transferred to Royal Air Force

Died: 02-06-1918 age 20

Peter was the eldest child of Captain James Joseph Rahill and his wife Margaret, who had married in Kilkenny in 1896. Their eldest child, Peter Joseph was born in Cork City, on 14 June 1897. The family moved to Chester around 1900 and it is here that the rest of their children, Mary Agnes, Austin, Francis, and Kathleen May were born. They were all baptised at St. Francis'. At first the family lived at 22 Whitefriars but by 1911 they had moved to 34 Gladstone Avenue.

The children attended St. Werburgh's Schools, even though they were living in St. Francis' Parish. However, Peter did not complete the whole of his education in Chester. He later transferred to the Franciscan College at Crescent Road, Cowley, near Oxford and was there when the 1911 census was taken. He must have come back to Chester soon afterwards because he stated on his enlistment papers that he worked as a clerk in the Army Accounts Department, Western Command, in Chester, from 1912 to 1915.

On 4 December 1915 Peter enlisted with the Royal Engineers at Chester, age 18. He gave his address as The Bungalow, Duke Street, Chester. His number was 142898. At some stage he transferred to the Cheshire Regiment and whilst with them he applied in 1917, to join the Royal Air Force. He gave his father James Joseph Rahill as his next of kin and his father's address as 8th Btn. Royal Defence Corps, Pearsons Park House, Hull.

Peter was posted to Reading, one of the two main training centres for flying officers, on 14 December 1917. He was stationed at the Infantry and Artillery School until 4 February 1918 when he became part of 37 Training Squadron. On 25 May 1918 he became a Flying Officer and was transferred as such to A and I.C.S. on 30 May 1918. His special qualifications were stated as Army Signal Instruction and French. Peter was killed on 2 June 1918 in a tragic flying accident at Worthy Down Aerodrome, near Winchester. This aerodrome was infamous for its challenging uphill landing sites.

Peter's body was brought to Chester for a requiem Mass in St. Francis' followed by interment on 6 June 1918 in Grave 561 at Overleigh Cemetery. The interment was attended by members of Peter's family and friends and also his fiancée, Miss Violet Foden. As Peter flew no missions abroad, he was not entitled to receive any campaign medals. His name is on the Memorial Board in Chester Town Hall and in St. Francis' Church, Chester.

James Herbert Roach

Pte. "E" Training Battalion Machine Gun Corps 178386

Died: 20-01-1919 age 29

James was the only child of John and Catherine Roach of Chester, who had both died before James enlisted. James married Elizabeth Campbell at St. Werburgh's before the start of the Great War and their three children, James Stanley, Elizabeth and Eleanor were also baptized there. James was employed by the London and North Western Railway, in Chester.

James' army records have survived and so we can piece together the complex moves of his military career. James enlisted on 19 June 1914, for 4 years with the Territorial Force in the U.K. His number was 1040. On his enlistment form James stated that he had spent 4 years with the Cheshire Brigade of the Royal Field Artillery. On 24 March 1915 James was posted to the reserves. He was then discharged 10 May 1915 as being medically unfit.

James then enlisted on 18 October 1915 with 3rd Battalion West Lancs. Kings Own Brigade No. 1924 at Edge Lane in Liverpool. On 14 June 1916 he was scheduled for Home Service only, due to his frequent attacks of asthma.

At some date, not shown James was then attached to The Royal Field Artillery TF 343 Brigade, Number 695447. He was declared medically unfit 22 June 1917 due to chronic asthma, and discharged 22 June 1917.

James was recalled to service, 4 November 1918, (695447) and died at the Military Hospital Cannock, 20 January 1919, from an abscess. He was brought back to Chester, where he was buried in Overleigh Cemetery Grave 282. As he did not serve abroad he would not have been entitled to any campaign medals. His name is on the Memorial Board in Chester Town Hall.

Lt. Edward Owen Roberts

Edward Owen Roberts

Lt. Royal Defence Force.

Died: 29-01-1917 age 48

Edward Owen Roberts was born c. 1869 in Llanfachreth, Merionethshire, Wales, the elder son of Owen Roberts and his wife Jane. Owen was a non-conformist minister and a yeoman farmer of substantial means. Nevertheless it must have been difficult for the family when Owen Roberts died, some time before 1881. His widow Jane then ran the farm herself, using hired labour.

Edward went to school in Aberystwyth and in 1891 Edward age 21, was a bar student in London and boarded with an assistant schoolmaster and his wife, in Camberwell. At the same time his brother John was a medical student. Edward was admitted to the Bar on 14 June 1893 and became a barrister on the Chester and North Wales circuit, attending Assizes and Quarter Sessions.

By 1901 the whole Roberts family had moved to Chester and lived at 140 Boughton. Jane was head of the family, with her sons Edward and John a barrister and a surgeon respectively. Three female servants made up the household.

At the same time Annie Grandidge was living with her sister, brother-in-law and their four children in Queen's Park, Chester. In 1903 Annie and Edward were married in Paddington, London. Afterwards the couple lived at The Grange, Hoole Road, Chester. The couple were not Catholic and had no children of their own but they were destined to play an important role in the lives of the children of St. Werburgh's Parish.

In 1905 Edward Owen Roberts represented Boughton as a Liberal Councillor on Chester City Council. He served on the Council until his death. From beginning to end of his civic career, he paid a great deal of attention to St. Werbergh's. In February 1906 Cllr. Owen Roberts visited the parish club and addressed the members and later in 1908 he again visited and gave a lecture. In July of 1908 the club was re-opened after a temporary closure for the fitting of electric light and consequent redecoration. Mrs. Owen Roberts officially turned on the new electric light and a vote of thanks was given by the club President Mr. Woods. Cllr. Owen Roberts responded.

By January 1907 Cllr. Owen Roberts had been appointed by the Council as a manager of St. Werburgh's Schools. There were six managers, including Canon Chambers, who was chairman. In July 1907 Cllr. Owen Roberts visited the Infants' School to distribute prizes, promising to return shortly to give prizes for drawing. Unfortunately his next recorded visit to the Infants' School was in November 1907 when he had to recommend that it should close until after the Christmas holidays due to an outbreak of measles in Chester. As promised, in July 1908 Cllr. and Mrs. Owen Roberts returned to give out six prizes for drawing, to six lucky children. The following day Mrs. Roberts returned alone to distribute cakes and sweets to all the children. At the same time Cllr. and Mrs. Owen Roberts were visiting the Girls' and Boys' Schools and awarding prizes for more advanced work such as essay writing.

Cllr. Owen Roberts remained a school manager until at least December 1916. During this time he displayed an identification with the aims and ideals of the schools which was amazing for someone of his background. He worked ceaselessly and tirelessly representing the views of the school managers to the City Council and promoting in every way he could the betterment of the schools, their staff and their children. His identification with the schools was very much above and beyond the call of duty. Cllr. and Mrs. Owen Roberts seemed to understand the difficulties which many of the children experienced and promoted their welfare in their civic roles.

At this time the parish was labouring under a tremendous debt, for both the upgrading of the schools and the completion of the church. Both projects involved huge sums of money which must have seemed inconceivable to the parishioners themselves. Owen Roberts provided a support in both these ventures and took an active part in fundraising and social activities within the parish e.g. in 1913 he contributed towards the stained glass memorial window to the deceased Infants' School Headmistress, Mother Elizabeth. By June 1914 both major building projects had been completed, though there was still a large outstanding debt.

The outbreak of war seemed to stimulate Edward Owen Roberts to even greater activity. He was somewhat old for initial volunteering or for conscription when it was introduced later. Instead he became one of the founders of the Chester Civilian Association. This body was involved in the drilling and training in rifle shooting of civilian Cestrians. Later it merged with the Cheshire Volunteer Regiment. Owen Roberts became the Hon. Sec. of the Chester and Eddisbury Battalion, with rank of sub-adjutant. He worked ceaselessly to further its aims, speaking at recruitment meetings in every part of the division. In 1915 he visited the trenches in France and from then on seemed to work even harder. In March 1916 he gained a commission in the Royal Defence Force. However he contracted an illness early in his military career which necessitated his treatment in a military hospital for some months. He then convalesced in Llandudno before gaining a promotion to a northern unit. However his illness recurred and he was brought home to Chester. Two weeks later, on 29 January 1917 Edward Owen Roberts died. Many thought that he had resumed military duties too soon after his first illness.

His funeral service was held at St. Paul's Anglican Church, Boughton. The coffin was then taken to Overleigh Cemetery for burial, with full military honours. Father Hayes from St. Werburgh's was one of those who walked behind the cortege to the cemetery. A full description of the funeral can be read in the Chester newspapers of the time. Wreaths sent by Fr. Hayes, St. Werburgh's CYMS, St. Werburgh's Schools and the Managers of St. Werburgh's Schools, were specifically mentioned.

In the February 1917 edition of St. Werburgh's Parish Magazine Canon Chambers wrote a fulsome obituary in which he stressed Mr. Owen Roberts' contribution to civic and parish life.

No mention was made of the fact that on 26 January, three days before his death, Edward Owen Roberts had been received into the Catholic Church by Fr. Maurice Hayes.

Private Michael Rogers

Michael Rogers

Pte. 1ˢᵗ Btn. Cheshire Regiment 8538

Died: 28-06-1917 age 27

Michael was the son of Michael and Ann Rogers nee Stanton. He was born on 20 February 1890 and baptised 6 April 1890 at St. Werburgh's. He was a middle child of a large family of children who grew up in the Boughton area of Chester. He attended St. Werburgh's schools.

Michael first enlisted with the Cheshire Regiment for a 7 and 5 year stint, on 1 July 1907, age 18 (slight exaggeration). He was one of four brothers who joined the Cheshires and all were bandsmen. In the early years of his service, Michael was posted several times to places within the U.K. including to Belfast. He transferred to the Reserves on 10 August 1912 and also married Martha Gault in Belfast the same year. Their first child, George was born in Belfast. By summer 1913 Michael had returned to Chester, where later their daughters, Ann and Winifred were born. All Michael and Martha Rogers' children were baptised at St. Werburgh's.

Since November 1913 Michael had been working as a postman in Chester (No.72467) but when war broke out he was immediately recalled to the Cheshire Regiment and landed at Le Havre on 16 August 1914 as part of the British Expeditionary Force in France. He was in C Company and was therefore at the first Battle of Mons. This ranked him with other "old contemptibles." One month later he was repatriated for hospital treatment. In total he carried out three periods of duty in France. Each of these periods ended with his being treated for gunshot wounds in Field or other Hospitals in France, followed by repatriation.

On 15 September 1914 he received gunshot wounds to the left foot, during the Battle of the Aisne. These were treated in a Field Hospital at Soissons and then in England at Carisbrooke Castle.

A further gunshot wound to the shoulder on 9 November 1915, received during the first Battle of Ypres, caused Michael to be sent to England via HMS "St. David."

In July 1916, gunshot wounds to feet and legs, received during the Battle of the Somme, resulted in his being sent to England per NS Stad Antwerpen.

During their father's periods of duty in France, Michael's two daughters, Ann and Winifred had died. Their deaths were the heartbreaking topic of letters between Martha Rogers and Michael's superior officer, as Martha did not wish her husband to suffer any further trauma by learning of these tragedies. Of course he did learn of them, eventually.

Michael returned to France after his last period of hospital treatment, with the rank of acting corporal. He joined the 1ˢᵗ Cheshires on 20 June 1917 at Ecurie Camp in the Reserve Area. In the afternoon of 27 June in a difficult and dangerous manoeuvre, the 1ˢᵗ Battalion Cheshires relieved 2ⁿᵈ Kings Own Scottish Borderers in front line trenches opposite Oppi Wood, during daylight. On 28 June they carried out an assault on Oppi Wood and Michael was probably one of the ten soldiers of other ranks who were killed in the action. Pte Michael Rogers was recorded as dead in the August 1917 issue of St. Werburgh's Parish Magazine.

Michael is buried in Orchard Dump Cemetery, Arleux-en-Gohelle, Pas de Calais, France – Grave VIII. A. 16. His name is also listed on the memorials in the Town Hall, Post Office, and St. Werburgh's Church, Chester. He was entitled to the 1914 Star with clasp, the British War Medal and the Allied Victory Medal.

Michael and Martha Rogers' second son, named Michael, was born posthumously, in 1918 and baptised at St. Werburgh's.

According to Chester newspaper reports, ten close members of Michael's family had enlisted at the time of his death. His step-father, who was also serving, had been wounded twice. Three brothers and three brothers-in-law were on active service, whilst one brother and one brother-in-law were prisoners of war in Germany.

John Rowlands

Pte. 1st Btn. King's Shropshire Light Infantry 7657

Died: 05-10-1914 age 27

The twins John and Selina Rowlands were two of the ten children born to John and Selina Rowlands nee McGiver of Chester, in July 1887. John was a Protestant shoemaker and a widower. Selina was a much younger Catholic girl, the daughter of Patrick Rowlands, also a Chester shoemaker. Their ten children were generally baptised first in an Anglican church and some time later, conditionally, in a Catholic Church, in Chester. Some of the children, like John and Selina, were baptised at St. Francis' and others were baptised at St. Werburgh's, depending on the address of the family at the time. During the 1880's the family lived in Watergate Street and in 1891 they lived in Royal Oak Yard.

Although ten children had been born, by 1901 four of them, Mary Elizabeth, Harriet, Elizabeth Ann and Patrick, had died in infancy. John snr. was also ill during these years and by 1911 the whole family had split up. William, the eldest child had joined the Royal Navy. John, Thomas, Elizabeth, and Joseph were living in the Chester workhouse and attending the school there, whilst Selina, John's twin sister, was at the Catholic Children's Home in Holywell. John snr. died in the workhouse in 1910.

In the 1911 census Selina was living at 15 Oswell Street, Rockferry with all her six children. William had returned from the Royal Navy and was working as a general labourer. John was working as a dock labourer and Thomas and Joseph were working as farm labourers. Selina was working as a housemaid and Elizabeth was still at school. Soon after this census the family probably moved back to Chester. (John's mother Selina certainly lived in Duke Street until her death in 1940.) Sadly John's twin sister Selina died in 1913 and was buried in Overleigh Cemetery. Also soon after this census, John must have enlisted with the King's Shropshire Light Infantry at Frodsham, as his four digit number was issued before the start of the Great War.

John's enlistment papers have not survived so we can know little of his army career. However, we know that as a regular soldier he would have been one of the first to go to France with the British Expeditionary Force. From the date and situation of his death we can deduce that he fell during the Battle of the Aisne. He may also have been involved in the preceding retreat from Mons and the Battle of the Marne.

Following the Allied victory at the Battle of the Marne in mid-September 1914, the German forces retreated to the high ground of the Chemin des Dames ridge on the north bank of the River Aisne. They dug trenches, (supported by heavy artillery) and prepared to fight.

The Allied attack started on the morning of 14 September and although there were some initial gains, as the day wore on the battle descended into a series of attacks and counter-attacks, with both sides suffering heavy casualties. By nightfall on 14 September, British units on the north bank of the river had been ordered to dig trenches and reinforce their positions, which now spanned a twenty mile front. Although the Battle of the Aisne continued for another ten days, neither side could claim a decisive victory. The German forces failed to drive the Allies back across the river, and the Allies were unable to push the Germans from the ridge. This 'stabilization' of the front marked the beginning of trench warfare – a gruelling stalemate that would last for almost four years.

It seems likely that John died during the action described above. He was buried in Grave I. B. 12 of Vailly-sur-Aisne British Cemetery and was entitled to receive the 1914 Star, the British War Medal and the Allied Victory Medal.

James Thomas Sharkey

Pte. 2nd Btn. Cheshire Regiment 8171

Died: 18-02-1915 age 25

James was born in Chester on 18 February 1890 and baptised at St. Francis Catholic Church, Chester on 7 December that year. He was the eldest child of James and Ann Sharkey nee Dennis. His father James was a labourer, who had come to Chester from Derbyshire, as a child. His mother Ann had been born in Chester. The family lived off Crook Lane, Watergate, Chester and each of their eight children was baptised at St. Francis.

James' army number indicates that he was a regular army soldier. In 1910 he married Louisa May Dew and the couple came to live at 23 Fosbrook Street, Boughton, in St. Werburgh's parish.

James' Medal Roll card reveals that he first went to France on 16 January 1915 and was killed in action there on 18 February 1915.

James Sharkey's death was recorded in the April 1915 edition of St. Werburgh's Parish Magazine. It seems ironic that he died on his 25th birthday.

James was eligible for the 1914–15 Star, the British War Medal and the Allied Victory Medal. His name is listed on the Ypres (Menin Gate) Memorial, West-Vlaanderen, Belgium, Panel 19–22. In Chester it is listed on the WW1 memorial in the Town Hall and that in St. Werburgh's Church.

Henry Siddall

Q.M. Sgt. Royal Army Medical Corps 19070

Died: 18-12-1918 age 33

Henry was the third of four children born to Henry and Mary Siddall nee Bray. His father Henry was an upholsterer and lived and worked at 126 Boughton. Henry had an elder brother William and elder sisters Mary Elizabeth and Margaret. He had been born on 23 July 1884 and baptised on 4 August 1884 at St. Werburgh's. Sadly Henry's mother died in 1887 when the family lived at 23 Boughton and was buried from St. Werburgh's. From then onwards Henry appears to have lived with his maternal grandmother and his mother's siblings.

Henry attended St. Werburgh's Schools and appears to have been an apt pupil. In the 1901 census Henry is living with his aunt, Louisa Bray, his late mother's youngest sister, at 26 Earl's Villas, City Road. Henry is 16 and working as a Grocer's Assistant. His father, who was living at 83 Boughton, died in July of that year.

Later Henry joined the R.A.M.C. and was trained as a dispenser. He was abroad in Mauritius and South Africa, with the R.A.M.C. at the time of the 1911 census.

As an already enlisted man, Henry entered France on 18 August 1914. His enlistment papers have not survived, so we have no details of his service. He must have been at home on leave in late 1915, because he married Ellen Butler at that time. She lived at 3 Albion Place, Chester.

Henry Siddall died at the 17th Casualty Clearing Station on 18 December 1918 and was buried in Charleroi Communal Cemetery, Grave P.8. He was entitled to receive the 1914 Star with clasp, the British War Medal and the Allied Victory Medal.

George Simmons

This name was on the original memorial plaque in St. Werburgh's, Chester.

It was not on the memorial board in Chester Town Hall.

The Commonwealth War Graves Commission lists three soldiers of this name, none of whom appear to have links to Chester or St. Werburgh's.

SIMMONS, GEORGE THOMAS

Rank: Corporal   **Service No**: 8063   **Date of Death**: 23/06/1915   **Age**: 26

Regiment/Service: Wiltshire Regiment, "B" Coy. Depot

Grave Reference: Screen Wall. F.B. 18. 130.

Cemetery: Wandsworth (Earlsfield) Cemetery

Additional Information: Son of Thomas and Mary Simmons, of Colerne, Wilts. Husband of Margaret C. Simmons of Gaulmilestown, Mullingar.

SIMMONS, ALFRED GEORGE

Rank: Corporal   **Service No**: 200871   **Date of Death**: 30/11/1917   **Age**: 20

Regiment/Service: Tank Corps "D" Bn.

Awards: MM

Grave Reference: XXX. N. 11A

Cemetery: Etaples Military Cemetery

Additional Information: Son of Alfred and Thirza Simmons, of St. Giles, Salisbury.

SIMMONS, GEORGE HENRY

Rank: Corporal   **Service No**: 14283 **Date of Death**: 03/11/1916   **Age**: 30

Regiment/Service: Norfolk Regiment, 8th Bn.

Panel Reference: Pier and Face 1 C and 1 D.

Memorial: Thiepval Memorial

Additional Information: Son of John and Hannah Simmons of 39, Neatherd Rd., Derhaln, Norfolk.

Vincent Stacey

Pte. 2ⁿᵈ Btn. Duke of Wellington's (West Riding) Regiment 9706

Died: 03-04-1915 age 24

Vincent Samuel Stacey was born in Chester in 1891, the third son of Samuel and Mary Stacey nee Rafferty. He was born on 17 April and baptised on 26 April at St. Francis. He had elder brothers Thomas and William and younger siblings Veronica Ann, John Leo and Mary Olive. All the siblings were baptised at St. Francis.

His father Samuel was an army pensioner and had been born in Yorkshire. His mother Mary had been born in Chester. Samuel and Mary had married in St. Werburgh's Chester on 28 October in 1884.

Samuel died in Chester in 1897 and Mary married Charles Waring in 1903. The family lived in Ashton-under-Lyne thereafter. It is here that Vincent married Florence Hanson at St. Anne's Church on 21 November 1912.

By the outbreak of war Vincent was living in Leeds and he enlisted in Halifax. His enlistment papers have not survived, so little is known of his short army life. However his roll medals reveal that he was sent to France on 20 January 1915. He was wounded and taken to No. 13 Station Hospital, Boulogne, where he died on 3 April 1915. His effects were transferred to his sole legatee, his wife Florence.

Vincent Stacey was recorded killed in action in the June 1915 edition of St. Werburgh's Parish Magazine. Vincent is buried in Grave III.D. 76. Boulogne Eastern Cemetery, France. He was entitled to the 1914–15 Star, the British War Medal and the Allied Victory Medal. His name is recorded on the WW1 memorials in the Town Hall and in St. Werburgh's and St. Francis' Churches, in Chester.

Driver Joseph Stretch

Joseph Stretch

Dvr. Royal Field Artillery, 3rd Brigade 735584

Died: 03-01-1918 age about 22.

This Chester family seems a likely one for Joseph Stretch.

Joseph was the only child born to Joseph and Mary Stretch nee Cooper. Joseph was a railway platelayer who had been born in Grappenhall, Lancashire and Mary had been born in Tarporley, Cheshire. Joseph had four older half siblings George, Jane, Arthur and Frederick, from his father's previous two marriages. In 1911 Joseph age 15 was the only child still living at home, 62 Trafford Street and was working as a hawker.

Joseph probably enlisted in early 1916 and had been serving abroad since July 1917. He contracted pneumonia whilst on active service in Palestine, in the Egyptian Theatre of War and was buried in Grave XIII.E.II. in Gaza War Cemetery. Joseph was entitled to receive the British War Medal and the Allied Victory Medal.

Joseph Stretch's name was on the original memorial in St. Werburgh's Church but sadly we have been unable to discover any connections between Joseph (or any other members of this family) and St. Werburgh's Parish.

Arthur Dennis Sullivan

Lce. Cpl 1st Btn. Cheshire Regiment 9519

Died: 22-10-1914 age 22

Arthur Dennis Sullivan was the eldest of 5 children born to Dennis and Mary Sullivan nee Lythgoe of Chester. Dennis was born in 1892 and had 4 younger brothers, William Henry, Frederick James, Albert Edward and Thomas Bernard. The family lived in Cuppin Street and all the children were baptised at St. Francis' Church. However, Dennis was confirmed at St. Werburgh's in 1905.

Dennis' number and rank indicates that he was probably already a member of the Cheshire Regiment when war broke out. His Commonwealth War Graves Commission data states that he had a wife, Bridget. It is possible that he and Bridget married in Belfast, just prior to Dennis being sent back from that posting to England when war broke out. Dennis' enlistment papers have not survived but his medal roll card indicates that he entered France on 27 August 1914. Sadly he was killed there on 22 October 1914, probably during the Battle of La Bassee which started on 10 October 1914 in the area around the Pas de Calais.

Dennis was entitled to receive the 1914 Star with clasp, the British War Medal and the Allied Victory Medal.

Dennis' name is listed on the Le Touret Memorial France, and the Memorial Board in the Town Hall Chester.

Andrew Sumpter

Pte. 10th Btn. Cheshire Regiment 35147

Died: 01-08-1917 age 26

Andrew was the son of Henry and Sarah Ann Sumpter nee Newton. The family was rooted in the Hoole area of the city, living successively in Faulkner Street, Panton Road, Brook Lane and Shavington Avenue. Andrew had two elder sisters, Elizabeth and Sarah and an elder brother, Henry. Andrew was educated at Arnold House School, situated on the corner of Parkgate Road and Walpole Street. This private school educated boys up to the age of 16, preparing them for public schools, Royal Navy, Sandhurst or the professions. The school closed in 1909.

Most of the Sumpter siblings worked in the family building business, which also employed several non-family workers. Andrew specialised in plumbing and his brother Henry in bricklaying. Their sister Elizabeth kept the accounts of the firm but Sarah started work as a pupil teacher in Chester at the age of 16.

On 11 December 1911 Andrew was received into the Catholic Church at St. Werburgh's and in 1912 he was confirmed here. Sometime between 1912 and 1914 he decided to try life in Australia as a dairy farmer. His parents also moved to Malcolm House, 1 Shavington Avenue, Newton-by-Chester.

When WW1 broke out Andrew returned from Australia in order to enlist, travelling on the SS 'Omrah' of the Orient Steam Navigation Company Lt. The ship left Brisbane and reached London on 21 June 1915. Andrew's father died in Chester on 5 November 1915 and Andrew then enlisted in 14th Cheshire Regiment at West Hartlepool on 10 December 1915. He was posted to Chester and then with the 10th Battalion of the Cheshires on the British Expeditionary Force to France, on 15 June 1916.

During his time in France, Andrew was plagued by minor medical ailments – perhaps as a result of the unhygienic state of life in the battalion. He was admitted at Field Ambulance 75 on 14 October 1916, for 6 days, to be treated for scabies. On 11 November 1916 he was admitted to Field Ambulance 77 for treatment for impetigo. He rejoined his battalion on 1 December 1916. Between then and 14 April 1917 he was admitted twice for infections which had caused defective vision and once for sickness. During July of 1917 Andrew was treated for ICT in both thighs.

He returned to duty on 27 July 1917 and then between 31 July and 4 August, the 10th Battalion was involved in the "minor" Battle of Pilckem Ridge, part of the greater Passchaendale confrontation. This was a particularly gruelling ordeal, with little trench warfare but fighting from mud-filled shell holes, during incessant rain, across open ground, under constant enemy shell fire, to prevent a German counter attack on the newly captured Bellewarde Ridge. When the 10th Battalion was relieved on the morning of 4 August one officer and 53 men were dead or missing. In addition 10 officers (of whom 6 remained on duty) and 140 men were wounded. Andrew was probably killed in action here on 1 August 1917, the first day of engagement with the enemy. His death was reported in an article in the October 1917 issue of St. Werburgh's Parish Magazine. In the article, it states that Canon Chambers had written a letter of condolence to Andrew's mother and relations, which had been gratefully acknowledged.

Andrew's mother died on 29 June 1918, so his effects together with his British War and Victory Medals were sent to his elder sister, Mrs. Elizabeth Ann Woolley of Wheatley Hill, County Durham.

Andrew's name is listed on the Ypres (Menin Gate) Memorial, West Vlaanderen, Belgium, Panel 19–22. In Chester it can be found on the Town Hall Memorial Board and the Arnold House Memorial Window in Chester Cathedral. It is also listed on the WW1 Memorial Boards in St. Werburgh's and in St. Francis' Catholic churches. In Hoole it is listed on the Memorial Board of All Saints Anglican Church and is engraved on the stone civic War Memorial at the corner of Kilmorey Park Road.

Corporal John Tatler

John Tatler

Cpl. 21ˢᵗ Btn. Manchester Regiment 19816

Died: 04/07-10-1917 age 26

John was the son of Charles and Catherine Tatler nee Donoghue, of 12 Love Street, Chester, who had been married at St. Werburgh's on 1 October 1888. John was born on 9 February 1891 and baptised on 1 March 1891 at St. Werburgh's. He was later confirmed here in 1905.

John was the eldest of three brothers and also had one elder sister, Elizabeth Agnes. Another sister, Margaret died age two years in August 1894 and was buried from St. Werburgh's. A third sister, Catherine Louise died in 1899 aged 7 months and was also buried from St. Werburgh's. In April 1901 their mother, Catherine died and was buried from St. Werburgh's. John's elder sister, Elizabeth Agnes appears to have acted as a mother figure to the boys as they grew up. In 1914 she married Arthur Adams and they came to live at 28 Love Street.

John's enlistment papers have not survived, so little is recorded of his army career. However it was recorded that John served with the British Expeditionary Force in France from 10 November 1915 until his death. Cpl. John Tatler was reported killed in action in the November 1917 issue of St. Werburgh's Parish Magazine.

A more complete description of his life and service was printed in the Cheshire Observer of Saturday 27 October 1917. It stated that his home was with his sister, Mrs. Adams of 28 Love Street and that before the war he was employed by Messrs. Taplen and Paddock, printers of Eastgate Row. He enlisted in January 1915 and had seen much fighting in 1916, during which he was wounded. After leave in July 1917 he returned to France, where he was killed in October. His apparently very amiable disposition attracted many friends both at home and throughout his army service. John's death was reported in the November 1917 issue of St. Werburgh's Parish Magazine.

John's medal roll card shows that he was entitled to the Allied Victory Medal, British War Medal and the 1914–15 Star.

His name is listed on the Tyne Cot Memorial, West-Vlaanderen, Belgium Panel 120–124, 162–162A and 163A. It is also recorded on the WW1 Memorial in the Town Hall and in St. Werburgh's Church, Chester.

Alexander Thompson

Pte. 2nd Btn. Cheshire Regiment 10428

Died: 03-10-1915

Although we cannot be certain, the Alexander Thompson described below would seem to be the one mentioned in St. Werburgh's Parish Magazine of October 1915 as having been killed in action.

Alexander's enlistment papers have not survived, so details of his army life are minimal. His medal roll card indicates that he entered France on 3 January 1915 and he died there on 3 October 1915. At this time the 2nd Battalion Cheshires were involved in heavy fighting in the West Face trench of the Hohenzollern Redoubt, during the Battle of Loos. The Hohenzollern Redoubt was a projecting earth work, strongly mined, to surround and protect a small hill known as the Dump, from which the enemy could observe the whole Rutoire plain. This redoubt had been captured and occupied by British troops but the enemy immediately started a counter attack. Movement in these shallow trenches was hampered by the presence of dead bodies and the enemy was much better equipped than the British troops. British losses had already reached high numbers and lack of efficient communication made receiving and carrying out orders almost impossible.

In the midst of this chaos the 2nd Cheshire Battalion was ordered to relieve the Royal Fusiliers on the West Face of the Hohenzollern Redoubt, on the night of 30 September 1915. Despite many problems, their occupation of the West Face trench was completed by 5.30am on 1 October 1915. Unfortunately enemy troops occupied three nearby connecting trenches. On the night of 1 October the Cheshires were ordered to mount an attack on one of these, the Chord. Their first attack was thought to have been successful, but such was the maze of trenches that this proved to be a false conclusion. Waves and waves of further attacks were ordered in the face of constant enemy bombing but the enemy were not moved. On 3 October the enemy attacked all along the West Face and gained a footing on the left of the Cheshires. All their bombers were killed. A bayonet counter attack was led by Major Roddy but met by bombs and the Cheshire soldiers were driven back to the British front line. Alexander could have been killed during any of the action on this day. On the night of 5 October the Cheshires were relieved by the 2nd Guards Brigade. During the whole action the 2nd Cheshire Battalion had lost 5 officers and 43 men and 7 officers and 153 men were wounded. 2 officers and 166 men were missing and were never recovered.

Alexander was entitled to the 1914–15 Star, the British War Medal and the Allied Victory Medal.

Andrew Charles Vahey

Lce. Cpl. South Wales Borderers 41641

Died: 11-04-1918 age 18

Andrew was the second child of Edward and Mary Ellen Vahey. Edward was a regular soldier who had been born in Lymm, Cheshire. Mary Ellen had been born in Birkenhead, as were Andrew and his elder brother Edward. Shortly after Andrew's birth in 1900 the family moved to Great Budworth, Cheshire, where younger brother Robert was born, and then to Tarvin where the remaining children of the family, Kathleen, Frederick and Dennis were born. By this time Edward had retired from the army and was working as a War Office messenger. All the children were still at school. The family would have been part of St. Werburgh's parish whilst living in both Budworth and Tarvin.

Because Andrew's enlistment papers have not survived, we know little of his army service. We only know that he was first with the Territorial Reserve Battalion and later transferred to the South Wales Borderers. His date of death and age at death, both raise doubts about his stated age on enlistment, which should have been at least 18 years.

Andrew was buried in Grave P. VII. K. 4A. St. Sever Cemetery Extension, Rouen.

His name is also listed on the Great War Memorial in Chester Town Hall. Andrew's medal roll card indicates that he was entitled to the British War Medal and the Allied Victory Medal.

Andrew's mother died in 1919 and his father in 1945. Both were buried in Overleigh Cemetery, Grave R687. Their address at that time was stated as Short Place, off Garden Lane, Chester.

Private Henry Vickers

Henry Vickers

Pte. 15th Btn. Lancashire Fusiliers 10265

Died: 01-07-1916 age 24 years

The Vickers were an old Cheshire family based in the village of Saughall, about five miles north of Chester. Joseph Vickers married Mary McLoughlin of Chester, in Chester, in 1889. Their family was to consist of four sons. Their first child, John Shepherd Vickers was born in 1891 and baptised at St. Werburgh's in Chester. Sadly he died in 1895 age four, when the family were living at 64 Cornwall Street.

Henry (Harry) was their next son. He was born on 29 June 1892 and baptised on 16 February 1893, at St. Werburgh's. He was to be the eldest of the three remaining brothers. By 1911 the family had moved to Seedley, Manchester and were working in engineering. The family attended St. James' Catholic Church in Pendleton.

Harry enlisted in November 1914 but little is known of his army career as his enlistment papers have not survived. However his Medal Roll Card states that he entered France on 23 November 1915. Pte. H. Vickers was reported killed in action in the August 1916 edition of St. Werburgh's Parish Magazine. He and his youngest brother Louis were killed on the same day. Their brother Percy had already been killed in the Dardanelles in 1915.

Harry was entitled to the 1914–15 Star, the British War Medal and the Allied Victory Medal.

Harry's name is listed on the Thiepval Memorial, Pier and Face 3C and 3D.

Private Louis Vickers

John Louis Vickers

Pte. 2/5 Btn. Royal Warwickshire Regiment 7321

Died: 01-07-1916 age 20

The Vickers was an old Cheshire family based in Saughall, about five miles north of Chester. Joseph Vickers married Mary McLoughlin of Chester, in Chester, in 1889. Their family was to consist of four sons. Their first child John Shepherd Vickers was born in 1891 and baptised at St. Werburgh's in Chester. Sadly he died in 1895 age four, when the family were living at 64 Cornwall Street.

John Louis was born on 13 August 1896 and baptised on 26 September 1896, at St. Werburgh's. He was the youngest of the three remaining brothers. By 1911 the family had moved to Seedley, Manchester and were working in engineering. The family attended St. James Catholic Church in Pendleton.

Although Louis enlisted first with the Lancashire Fusiliers he was later transferred at some stage to the Royal Warwickshire Regiment. Louis' enlistment papers have not survived, so little is known of this move, or indeed of most of his army career.

Pte. L. Vickers was reported killed in action in the August 1916 edition of St. Werburgh's Parish Magazine. Tragically, Louis was one of 3 brothers who all died in this conflict, Louis and Harry Vickers dying on the same day. He was entitled to receive the British War Medal and the Allied Victory Medal.

Louis Vickers is buried in Grave 1. J.13 Rue-du-Bacquerot No.1 Military Cemetery, Laventie, Pas de Calais, France.

Private Percy Vickers

Percy Joseph Vickers

Pte. 1/7 Btn. Lancashire Fusiliers 2003

Died: 20-12-1915 age 22 years

The Vickers were an old Cheshire family based in Saughall, about five miles north of Chester. Joseph Vickers married Mary McLoughlin of Chester, in Chester, in 1889. Their family was to consist of four sons. Their first child John Shepherd Vickers was born in 1891 and baptised at St. Werburgh's in Chester. Sadly he died in 1895 age four, when the family were living at 64 Cornwall Street.

Percy Joseph was born on 28 June 1893 and baptised on 22 August 1893, at St. Werburgh's. He was the middle in age of the three remaining brothers. By 1911 the family had moved to Seedley, Manchester where Percy was employed in the engineering firm of Messrs. Smith and Coventry. The family attended St. James' Catholic Church in Pendleton.

Percy's enlistment papers have not survived so little is known of his army career. Tragically, Percy Joseph was one of 3 brothers who died in this conflict. His two brothers, Louis and Henry died less than a year later on the same day. Percy was entitled to receive the 1914–15 Star, the British War Medal and the Allied Victory Medal.

Percy's name is listed on the Helles Memorial, Turkey (Gallipoli) Panel 58–72 or 218–219.

Thomas Waldron

Pte. Kings Own Royal Lancaster Regiment and Royal Engineers 7494–24644

Died: 12-12-1916 age 31

Thomas was the eldest of 11 children (six of whom died young) born to Patrick and Mary Waldron nee Moran, of Chester. Thomas was born on 15 May 1885 and was baptised at St. Werburgh's on 14 June that year. He was later confirmed at St. Werburgh's in July 1899.

In the 1901 census the family lived at 20 Steam Mill Street. Later the family moved to 23 Seaville Street and later to 31 Victor Street.

Thomas enlisted at Frodsham in the King's Own Royal Lancaster Regiment on 16 September 1902, when he was 18 years and six months. He had already been in the 3rd Cheshire Regiment. He served at home until 9 February 1904, when he sailed for India. Thomas was in India for over 7 years, until 31 October 1911. During this time he received a 1st and then a 2nd class education certificate and passed a gun drill course. Whilst in Calcutta, in 1909, he passed a telegraphy course and became an Office Telegraphist.

During this time Thomas had gained two good conduct medals and there were no complaints or charges laid against him. However, the next section of Thomas' army records, outline a different story. He was twice reported for basically using the telegraphic equipment for holding "private communications." The temptation to "chat" was obviously too great for him to withstand.

On 24 May 1913 Thomas was transferred to the Royal Engineers and on 8 September 1914 his unit went with the British Expeditionary Force to France. He was predominantly engaged in telegraphic work but nevertheless was admitted to 18th Field Ambulance on 22 August 1915, with abrasions to the right ankle. He was discharged to duty after 7 days. A year later, on 8 July 1916 Thomas was to be admitted to hospital again, this time for more serious reasons. On 28 July 1916 he was transferred to the 8th Stationary Hospital and returned to England.

Thomas was discharged on 7 September 1916 as being medically unfit. His army medical report states that he was suffering from Pulmonary Tuberculosis. This had started in France on 7 July 1916 and he had lost 2 stone in weight since that date. The bacillus was present in urine and sputum and caused coughing and night sweats. The onset was said to be the result of active service exposure and left Thomas with total permanent incapacity.

Three months later Thomas died at home in Chester and was buried in Overleigh Cemetery, Grave 11155. His fulsome obituary was printed in St. Werburgh's Parish Magazine of January 1917. Thomas was entitled to the 1914 Star, the British War Medal and the Allied Victory Medal. His name is listed on the memorial in Chester Town Hall.

Michael Walsh

Pte. 5th Siege Company, Royal Engineers, Royal Monmouthshire 6071

Died: 07-01-1916 at Gallipoli, possibly age 35

His grave is III.F.168 East Mudros Military Cemetery, Lemnos Island, Greece.

Michael's name was on the original Memorial Plaque at St. Werburgh's and therefore will be inscribed on any new Memorial Plaque placed there.

A possible family in the parish was that of Michael and Bridget Mary Walsh of 7 Steam Mill Street. Michael snr. was a nursery gardener. By 1911 seven children had been born to the couple but only two had survived, Michael and his younger brother John. Michael had possibly been in the army since about 1900 as he did not appear in Steven Street on any census after 1891 but there is no record of his death.

Corporal Thomas Ward

Thomas Ward

Cpl. 1ˢᵗ Btn. Royal Welsh Fusiliers 4375

Died: 21-05-1915 age 22

Thomas was the son of Michael Ward who had been born in Galway but later moved to Chester. Here Michael married Ellen Coriam at St. Werburgh's in 1888. The couple lived at 5 Steven Street, though later they moved to number 22. Thomas was the second of their six children and was born on 16 September 1892. He was baptised at St. Werburgh's on 2 October 1892 and later confirmed there in 1905. Thomas attended St. Werburgh's Schools and was by reputation, an apt pupil. After leaving school at the age of 14, he worked at the lead works in Boughton. He apparently wished to emigrate to America, the goal of many youngsters at that time but history intervened.

When war broke out Thomas enlisted at Wrexham in September 1914. Anecdotal evidence states that all available men from Steven Street got on a bus going from Chester to Wrexham, in order to enlist together. Most of them would have been members of this parish, as the population of Steven Street was allegedly 99% Catholic at this time.

After initial training Thomas was sent to France and Flanders. His army papers have not survived, so there are few details of his service available. He embarked with the regiment and entered France on 2 November 1914. It was there that he was promoted to Corporal, prior to being killed in action at Frezenberg Ridge. He died on 21 May 1915 and his name is listed on Le Touret Memorial, Pas de Calais, France, Panel 13 and 14. It is also on the WW1 memorial in the Town Hall and in St. Werburgh's Church, Chester. Thomas was entitled to the 1914 Star, the British War Medal and the Allied Victory Medal.

Sgt. Wilfred Warren & his three sons

Wilfred Joseph Warren

Sgt. 80th Field Company, Royal Engineers 42990

Died: 30-10-1917 age 29

Wilfred was the son of Richard and Mary Warren and was born in Wavertree, Liverpool in 1887. He was the youngest of five children. By 1891 the family had moved to Chester, where Richard worked as a Railway Fireman. The family first lived in West Street and later in Ivy Terrace. Wilfred became an engineering apprentice at the Hydraulic Engineering Works and was well known as a local amateur footballer.

Wilfred married Catherine Malone at St. Francis, Chester in 1908 and they lived at 7 New Crane Street. Their first two sons Thomas Richard and Wilfred Joseph were baptised at St. Francis. The family later moved to 39 St. Mark's Terrace, Saltney and were living there when their third son, Thomas James was born.

By 1911, the family had moved to Manchester, where Wilfred worked as a machinery engineer at Hall Bridge Engineering Works, Castleton and the family lived in Castle Fields. Sadly Catherine died in 1911 and was buried in grave R610 of Overleigh Cemetery, Chester on 9 August. It seems likely that the three boys were brought up by their Malone relatives in Chester. Richard and Joseph attended St. Anthony's Infant School, Saltney and then St. Werburgh's Boys' Junior School, until they left age 14. Thomas James also attended St. Werburgh's Schools. During this time they lived with their guardian, Agnes Malone at Glen Aber Cottage, Saltney.

Wilfred's enlistment papers have not survived and so no official details of his service are recorded. However, the Chester Chronicle of 24 November 1917 stated that he joined up in August 1914. Family information tells us that Wilfred sent letters and postcards home to his three sons, all the time he was in France. He was particularly anxious to keep in contact with his youngest son. He also kept detailed notebooks about the machinery he used and the best way to maintain it. This was so that all members of his unit could benefit from his expertise.

It had been recorded in the June 1915 issue of St. Werburgh's Parish Magazine that Wilfred Warren had enlisted in an army transport unit and the Chester Chronicle stated that he was in France for two years and three months prior to his death. During this time he had twice received certificates from his Sergeant-Major commending his division for gallantry and devotion to duty. St. Werburgh's Parish magazine reported in the December 1917 issue, that Sgt. Wilfred Warren had been killed in action. He was with the 80th Transport Company of the Royal Engineers. A letter sent to Mrs. Miller, his sister and next of kin, from his Commanding Officer stated that he had never lost a better or more valuable N.C.O.

Wilfred was entitled to the 1914–15 Star, the British War Medal and the Allied Victory Medal. He is buried in grave V.B.31 Bard Cottage Cemetery, West-Vlaanderen Belgium. The grave is under the care of the Commonwealth War Graves Commission. Wilfred's name is listed on the WW1 memorials in St. Werburgh's and St. Francis' Church in Chester.

Constant Wauters

Soldaat, First Line Infantry, Belgian Army 2KLBV1906

Died: 11-03-1915 age 26

Constant was born in Gent, Belgium on 25 December 1888. His address on enlisting was Martelarenlaan 355, Gent. Constant and other Belgian soldiers had been treated together with British soldiers in a medical facility in France. They were then all sent on a hospital train to England. Constant arrived in England in October 1914 and was sent eventually to Richmond House, 123 Boughton, Chester, which was a private house turned into an auxiliary hospital for the duration of the war. It was the main centre for injured Belgian soldiers in Cheshire and also housed some British soldiers. Persons sent on the hospital trains were thought to have a good chance of surviving nevertheless his time here must have been difficult for Constant, as his wife and two small children remained in Belgium. Constant was originally suffering from a severe wound. Initially the wound appeared to be healing well and it was thought that he might eventually be discharged. However, meningitis later set in.

Constant was seriously ill for about six weeks and unconscious for about fourteen days. During this time, nuns from the Little Sisters of the Assumption Convent in Chester sat with him night and day, in order to take care of his needs and to release other nurses for duty on the rest of the ward. Constant died on the morning of Thursday 11 March 1915. His coffin was received into St. Werburgh's Church on Friday evening and lay there overnight. His funeral was conducted on Saturday 13 March with full military honours. A Requiem Mass was sung at 10.00am, the coffin covered by the Belgian colours and resting before the high altar. The celebrant was Father Loos, a Belgian priest who was resident at St. Werburgh's at this time and who served the Belgian refugee population of Chester and surrounding area. All Belgian refugees throughout the north-west appear to have made their way to St. Werburgh's and after the mass Fr. Loos addressed the congregation in Flemish and French. During the morning many Cestrians came to pay their respects at the coffin, which eventually became covered with wreaths. Lady Mackinnon brought a wreath from Government House and the local Red Cross sent a cross of red roses on a white blossom background. The Cheshire Regiment sent a laurel wreath tied with the Belgian colours. Alongside these was placed a wreath of violets from Constant's wife.

At 2.45pm the funeral procession left the church, accompanied by four priests, Canon Chambers (rector), Fr. Hayes, Fr. O'Hara and Fr. Loos. The coffin was conveyed to Overleigh Cemetery on a transport wagon draped with the national flags. The local Artillery Corps provided four horses to pull the wagon. The Depot band played funeral marches and the Depot also provided a firing party. The military procession included detachments from the Depot, the 5th Cheshire, the Artillery and the Yeomanry. Crowds of respectful spectators lined the streets. Fr. Loos officiated at the interment in Grave 11864.

This funeral was the first and only funeral of a Belgian combatant to take place in the Chester area and Constant's grave is the only grave of a Belgian combatant to be found in Overleigh Cemetery.

Charles Henry White

Lce. Cpl. 1ˢᵗ Btn. Border Regiment 34931

Died: 22-08-1918 age 31

Charles Henry White was born in Churton, Cheshire, the son of William White who was a farm labourer and his wife Jane. He had 9 siblings, two of whom died before 1911. His elder siblings were George and John and younger siblings were Frederick, Annie, Elizabeth, Arthur, Frank and May. Charles' elder brothers became farm workers and in 1901 Charles worked for Joseph Johnson, a building contractor in Rossett and lived there with this family.

On 15 April 1905 Charles enlisted with the Army Service Corps at Chester, as a driver. His enlistment papers state that he is Anglican. He served for two years, being stationed in Manchester, at Longford and at the Curragh and left with good reports as to his conduct and proficiency as a driver and groom. He was then transferred to the reserves, with his intended address given as Churton, Cheshire. In the 1911 census, he had returned to his family in Churton and working there as a farm labourer.

As a reservist, Charles was mobilized on 6 August 1914 was sent to France on 7 September and joined 21ˢᵗ Field Ambulance Company on 17 September. At first his army career went smoothly, with promotions to Lance Corporal and Corporal but on 15 August 1915 he was demoted to driver as punishment for some minor misconduct and his career then followed a bumpy track for the next couple of years. There were disciplinary incidents in November and December 1915. Eventually Charles was granted leave from 28 December 1915 until 4 January 1916. He returned to Chester and married Mary Ellen Nicholson at Chester Register Office on 4 January 1916, before returning immediately to France. The couple already had a baby son, Francis White Nicholson, who had been born on 22 March 1915.

Charles' next few months of army service were also of a variable nature. In May he absented himself without leave for 9 days, before giving himself up. He was tried on 17 May and received a sentence of 6 months imprisonment which was suspended. Charles was admitted to hospital on 23 May with appendicitis and discharged on 2 June 1916. He returned to duty with the 21ˢᵗ Field Ambulance unit.

The rest of the year was uneventful but by 17 February he was again awaiting trial for being absent without leave for 8 days. This time he was sentenced to a year's imprisonment. Six months were immediately remitted and the remaining six months suspended, under a special wartime protocol. However, he was transferred to the Border Regiment and reduced to pay as a private soldier.

Life in the infantry seemed to suit Charles better and he progressed without incident, being promoted to Lance Corporal in October 1917. On 21 November 1917 he was treated for a gunshot wound in the leg at Rouen and on 13 December he returned to duty. On 16 December 1917 his suspended sentences were remitted.

We must now assume that Charles received some leave, because on 3 January 1918 he and Mary Ellen nee Nicholson had a religious marriage ceremony at St. Werburgh's; the same church in which Mary Ellen had been baptised. Their address was 11 Tomkinson Street, Hoole. Soon after the ceremony Charles returned to France.

On 11 January 1918 Charles was awarded the D.C.M. for conspicuous gallantry and devotion to duty. In the citation printed in the London Gazette of 1 May 1918 it stated that "When the enemy made a determined effort to outflank our troops, he lead his Lewis gun team to the exposed flank and brought heavy fire to bear on the enemy, checking their advance. Though badly wounded he remained in action until ordered to leave the firing line. He showed great courage and determination."

On 19 August 1918 Charles was wounded in action and died of those wounds on 22 August. His widow, Mary Ellen White received his effects, which consisted of his wallet and cash, letters, photographs, cards, a religious book, medal ribbons, a cap badge, a Sacred Heart Badge, stamps, false teeth, a cigarette case and a rosary. She was living at this time at her grandparents' home, the London Bridge Hotel, Chester. By 1920 when Charles' medals were sent, she had moved to 2 Stanley Street, Chester.

Charles was buried in Grave V.D.82 Longuenesse (St. Omer) Souvenir Cemetery. He was awarded the 1914 Star, the British War Medal, the Allied Victory Medal and the Distinguished Conduct Medal.

His name is on the Great War Memorial Board in Chester Town Hall.

Private William Henry Whitley

William Henry Whitley

Pte. 12th Btn. Cheshire Regiment 13606

Died: Salonica, Serbia 25-04-1917 age 30

William was born in Chester in 1887, the son of William and Elizabeth Ann Whitley nee Coppack and grew up with his ten siblings, at 11 Parkgate Road. By 1911 his father had died, as had three of his siblings and three other siblings had left home. The family at Parkgate Road then consisted of his mother, his elder brother Thomas with his wife Maria, and his three younger siblings, Robert Charles, Florence Mary and Edith Amelia. William himself, age 23 was working as a general labourer. In 1913 he married Catherine Gerraghty, first in a civil ceremony and afterwards at St. Werburgh's. The couple's daughter, Margaret Mary was born on 6 September 1914 and baptised shortly afterwards at St. Werburgh's.

William had already enlisted at Chester on 31 August, 1914 and was posted on 5 September 1914 for military training near Aldershot. William Henry Whitley was received into the Catholic Church at St. Werburgh's on 26 August 1915. He then received his posting to France, sailing on 6 September 1915 from Folkestone to join the British Expeditionary Force. Scarcely had he arrived, than on 28 October 1915 he embarked at Marseille as part of the Mediterranean Expeditionary Force in the Balkans. William would have joined the British Forces confronting the Bulgarians along the Doiran Front. This was a stretch of trenches and fortifications along the valley of the River Vardar and bordering Lake Doiran.

There was a British attack along this front in August 1916. This had been surprisingly well-resisted by the Bulgarians and thereafter the military situation was not especially active until April of 1917. The British then advanced upon Bulgarian lines in order to rationalise the trench positions on the section around Kidney and Horseshoe Hills. In April 1917 William would have been with the 12th Cheshires at Kidney Hill. On 23 April 1917, the 12th Battalion Cheshires moved to Horseshoe Hill to support the 13th Btn. Manchester Regiment. The Manchester Regiment had achieved all its objectives by 25 April, supported throughout by artillery bombardment from the 12th Battalion Cheshires. However, the whole of this Sector was heavily shelled by the enemy during this day, especially during a counter attack at 12.00 hours. It is probable that William was killed by this shellfire, on 25 April 1917. The British withdrew to their initial positions on 27 April 1917. Further military action occurred in May 1917. These engagements are referred to as the Battles of Doiran or the Vardar.

The death of Pte. William Whitley was recorded in the June 1917 issue of St. Werburgh's Parish Magazine and at the end of 1917 his widow Catherine was awarded 18 shillings and nine pence per week on which to support herself and her child. The family were living in Seaville Street, Chester at this time. However, Catherine died in 1918. Because of this, it was Mrs. Margaret

Hodson, of Steam Mill Street, who received William's medals etc. on behalf of her niece, Margaret Mary Whitley, age 6. The medals consisted of 1914–15 Star, British War Medal and Allied Victory Medal.

William is buried in grave F. 1412, Karasouli Military Cemetery, Greece. His name is listed on the WW1 memorial in the Town Hall and also in St. Werburgh's Church, Chester.

The History and Mystery of the War Memorial Chapel, St. Werburgh's Catholic Church, Chester

As early as December 1917 Canon Chambers, the rector of St. Werburgh's since 1903, proposed in the Parish Magazine the building of a memorial to the parishioners who had given their lives in the Great War. At this time the outcome of the war was by no means certain but whichever way events were to play out, Canon Chambers was convinced that the parish of St. Werburgh, which had already made so many sacrifices during this war (and was to make still more) should have a memorial to commemorate them. In his opinion the memorial should be a side altar portraying Our Lady of Sorrows and in this chapel should be placed a plaque carrying the names of the fallen men.

Canon Chambers felt that only persons who had lived in the parish or been benefactors of it should be named on the plaque and that the family proposing a name should donate a sum of perhaps £1. I feel sure that this subscription idea was not strictly adhered to in the ensuing years. There were persons named on the memorial whose families could not possibly have afforded such a sum. On the other hand there were generous donors who probably paid more than the quoted £1.

After 1917 no more magazines were published, probably due to paper rationing. Newspapers also were curtailed e.g. Cheshire Observer fell from around 18 pages to around 4 during this period. However, we can surely imagine without written evidence, the rejoicing which was experienced in the parish when the guns fell silent on 11 November 1918 as the Armistice was signed and when the Peace Treaty of Versailles was signed on 28 June 1919. Perhaps those celebrating most were the children, who were given a day off school on each occasion[1]!

We can also imagine the mixed feelings of those families to whom a father or son was not to return. There must have been much planning and fundraising within the parish during the next few years, so that the Memorial Chapel and Plaque to the fallen, could be realised. These activities culminated in a letter sent from Canon Chambers to the architectural firm of Edmund Kirby and Sons of Liverpool, on 5 April 1921. Edmund Kirby was the architect who had originally designed St. Werburgh's Church. Kirby died in 1920 and his son Edmund Bertram Kirby was the recipient of this letter. In it, Canon Chambers asks Bertram Kirby to design an altar for the Great War Memorial Chapel. He wishes the altar to be in red sandstone, with a Pieta relief in white stone or plaster. He also mentions that Hardman's of Birmingham have received a commission to make a plaque, with the names of 96 fallen parishioners upon it. He expected the plaque to arrive in another two months and it had certainly been placed on the wall of what was to become the War Memorial Chapel, by October 1922.

A letter sent by Canon Chambers to Bertram Kirby on 11 October 1922 then asks Kirby to now design a cavity in the altar. The cavity should be large enough to contain a bottle enclosing a scroll listing the 96 names. Apparently he had promised this to the families who wanted their loved ones named. He said that the 96 names represented 96 grieving mothers and was most insistent that Kirby should include a cavity in the design of the altar. Kirby apparently completed this extra task and Canon Chambers congratulated him later, saying that the whole church of St. Werburgh was a tribute to both his father and himself[2].

The altar and plaque having been installed, on 15 September 1923 the Great War Memorial Chapel was dedicated at a High Mass celebrated by Hugh Singleton, Roman Catholic Bishop of Shrewsbury. The Cheshire Observer of 22 September 1923 carried a lovely picture of the Memorial Chapel and an article about the dedication. It was apparently the first Great War Memorial to be placed within a Chester Church. The Chester Chronicle carried a description of the Memorial Chapel and almost the full text of the sermon preached at the dedication ceremony! The Memorial Chapel was described in glowing terms and the altar as a whole was said to be an exquisite sculpture and an asset to the City of Chester[3].

However, the fate of the memorial plaque has not been so fortunate. It was wrought by Hardman and Co. of Birmingham, the premier metal workers of the day, who had also produced most of the stained glass and metalwork within St. Werburgh's Church. Sadly, during some restructuring work in the church post WW2, the plaque was lost. This was a tragedy for the parishioners of St. Werburgh's.

In the 1980's Fr. Lloyd, an assistant priest at St. Werburgh's tried to reconstitute the list of names which had been on the plaque. This was a complex and extremely difficult task. It involved trying to contact living relatives of past parishioners and asking help from the Cheshire Military Museum and any other bodies who might have information. Internet access to some records was not as freely available as it is today but Fr. Lloyd and his team eventually compiled a list of 68 names. (They probably did not know the story of the 96 names in the altar cavity.) The 68 names were written in illuminated text on card and placed in a frame in the Memorial Chapel. Joseph Gray, Roman Catholic Bishop of Shrewsbury officiated at the dedication ceremony in 1990[4].

We now fast forward to 2013. Many citizens and Government officials felt that in the year of the centenary of the start of the Great War, commemorative events or activities should take place. Local History Societies were asked to promote these and many chose to undertake research into the names on the memorials in different parts of the country. It seemed as though this could be feasible for St. Werburgh's, if a group of interested people could get together to engage in the work. 68 are a great many names to research! Fr. Paul Shaw was very supportive of the idea and a group of interested parishioners started work. Their efforts were rewarded when the biographical details of the 68 parishioners who died in the Great War were placed on our parish website. Seven more persons were discovered whose names should have been on the list but were not placed there in 1990. This brought the total to 75.

War Memorial Chapel, St. Werburgh's Catholic Church, Chester

During the research phase, two of the study group went to visit the Liverpool Records Office, where the papers of Edmund Kirby and Sons have been deposited. They were delighted to find there, the letters previously described, between Canon Chambers and Bertram Kirby, about the War Memorial Chapel and the scroll of 96 names. Unfortunately this meant that they now had at least 21 more names to find and research! It also meant that the full original list of fallen men was buried within the altar but there was no way of reaching it and discovering the names. So near and yet so far!

More new names for the memorial were suggested and checked out but there seemed no way that the mystery of the full list of original names on the plaque could ever be solved. Then internet research revealed that the Hardman archives had been deposited in the Wolfson Archive Centre of Birmingham Library. Much of the firm's archive material had been destroyed by a fire in Hardman's premises but the remainder was in Birmingham Library. It seemed too much to hope that records of the St. Werburgh's items would be preserved. Against all the odds however, it was found that the order form for the original St. Werburgh's Great War Memorial Plaque was intact. On the order form was a list of the 96 names which Canon Chambers had mentioned. There was also a description of the plaque and its inscriptions[5]. What a bonanza!

In a separate file there was discovered a letter from Canon Chambers to Hardman's, yet again requesting an alteration. Apparently the rather frail mother of a fallen soldier had not been able to get down to St. Werburgh's in time to put her son's name on the list. Canon Chambers was concerned that it should be added. By this time the plaque was complete and had been hung in St. Werburgh's. Hardman's agreed to make an additional piece of bronze with the name of James Francis Kelly inscribed, which could be added to the original plaque. The plaque had cost £100 for the 96 names, roughly £1 per name. The name of James Francis Kelly cost over £3[6]!

The discovery of what we came to call the Hardman List allowed us to compare the names listed on the original memorial, the 1990 memorial and those gathered during the 2014 research period. As had been suspected, a few names on the 1990 memorial were not valid, most of the newly gathered names were and 34 completely new names had been found on the original memorial. This brings the total number of names for any new WW1 memorial in St. Werburgh's, to 115.

Today in the War Memorial Chapel there are also lists of parishioners who died in WW2, Korea, Northern Ireland and Afghanistan. The altar of red sandstone, with its contrasting white Pieta, is still stunning and provides a place where parishioners can remember and pray for service personnel lost in all wars and their families. It is special in many ways but particularly in the way that the names of its original Great War dead were first gathered, then lost and then, after two attempts, found again.

References

1 Log Book of St. Werburgh's Girls' School, ZDES 47 Cheshire and Chester Archives and Local Studies, Duke Street, Chester.

2 Deposit of Edmund Kirby and Sons, 720KIR/872 Liverpool Records Office, St. George's Square.

3 Chester Chronicle, 21 September 1923, Cheshire and Chester Archives and Local Studies, Duke Street, Chester.

4 Leaflet re. Dedication of WW1 Memorial 1990 held at St. Werburgh's, Chester.

5 Order 181, Hardman Order Book for 1920–22, MS 175/A/4/3/9/10 Archives, Birmingham Library.

6 Miscellaneous letters in Hardman Archives, MS 175/A/4/3/9/10 Birmingham Library.

Ann Marie Curtis April 2014.

THE FOLLOWING PHOTOGRAPHS SHOW MILITARY CEMETERIES AND MEMORIAL GARDENS ADMINISTERED BY THE COMMONWEALTH WAR GRAVES COMMISSION WHICH ARE REFERENCED IN THE BIOGRAPHIES.

THEY ARE REPRODUCED HERE BY KIND PERMISSION OF CWGC.

Arras Memorial

Arras Flying Services Memorial

Baghadad (North Gate) War Cemetery

Bagneaux British Cemetery, Gezaincourt

Bailleul Communal Cemetery Extension, Nord

Beacon Cemetery, Sailly-Laurette

Beaurevoir Communal Cemetery British Extension

Bois-Grenier Communal Cemetery

Boulogne Eastern Cemetery

Brown's Copse Cemetery, Roeux

Bucquoy Road Cemetery, Ficheux

Charleroi Communal Cemetery

Cite Bonjean Military Cemetery, Armentieres

Doullens Communal Cemetery Extension No. 1

Dozinghem Military Cemetery

East Mudros Military Cemetery

Faubourg D'amiens Cemetery, Arras

Favreuil British Cemetery

Flatiron Copse Cemetery, Mametz

Gaza War Cemetery

Grove Town Cemetery, Meaulte

Hamel Military Cemetery, Beaumont-Hamel

Heilly Station Cemetery, Mericourt-L'abbe

Helles Memorial

Kantara War Memorial Cemetery

Karasouli Military Cemetery

La Ferte-Sous-Jouarre Memorial

La Neuville British Cemetery, Corbie

Le Touret Memorial

Lijssenthoek Military Cemetery

Longuenesse (St. Omer) Souvenir Cemetery

Orchard Dump Cemetery, Arieux-En-Gohelle

Passchendaele New British Cemetery

Ploegsteert Memorial

Plovdiv Central Cemetery

Plymouth Naval Memorial

Pont-Du-Hem Military Cemetery, La Gorgue

Poole Cemetery

Ramleh War Cemetery

Rue-Du-Bacquerot No. 1 Military Cemetery, Laventie

Soissons Memorial

Spoilbank Cemetery

St. Sever Cemetery Extension, Rouen

Sucrerie Cemetery, Ablain-St. Nazaire

Terlinchthun British Cemetery, Wimille

Thiepval Memorial

Tower Hill Memorial

Tyne Cot Memorial

Vailly British Cemetery

Valenciennes (St. Roch) Communal Cemetery

Verchain British Cemetery, Verchain-Maugre

Vis-En-Artois Memorial

Wimereux Communal Cemetery

Ypres (Menin Gate) Memorial

Ypres, Bard Cottage Cemetery

Zantvoorde British Cemetery